ON ANGER

Seneca

Translated by Aubrey Stewart in 1900.

Table of Contents

BOOK 1 3
BOOK 2 39
BOOK 3 88

BOOK 1

I.
YOU have demanded of me, Novatus, that I should write how anger may be soothed, and it appears to me that you are right in feeling especial fear of this passion, which is above all others hideous and wild: for the others have some alloy of peace and quiet, but this consists wholly in action and the impulse of grief, raging with an utterly inhuman lust for arms, blood and tortures, careless of itself provided it hurts another, rushing upon the very point of the sword, and greedy for revenge even when it drags the avenger to ruin with itself. Some of the wisest of men have in consequence of this called anger a short madness: for it is equally devoid of self control, regardless of decorum, forgetful of kinship, obstinately engrossed in whatever it begins to do, deaf to reason and advice, excited by trifling causes, awkward at perceiving what is true and just, and very like a falling rock which breaks itself to pieces upon the very thing which it crushes. That you may know that they whom anger possesses are not sane, look at their appearance; for as there are distinct symptoms which mark madmen, such as a bold and menacing air, a gloomy brow, a stern face, a hurried walk, restless hands, changed colour, quick and strongly-drawn breathing; the signs of angry men,

too, are the same: their eyes blaze and sparkle, their whole face is a deep red with the blood which boils up from the bottom of their heart, their lips quiver, their teeth are set, their hair bristles and stands on end, their breath is laboured and hissing, their joints crack as they twist them about, they groan, bellow, and burst into scarcely intelligible talk, they often clap their hands together and stamp on the ground with their feet, and their whole body is highly-strung and plays those tricks which mark a distraught mind, so as to furnish an ugly and shocking picture of self-perversion and excitement. You cannot tell whether this vice is more execrable or more disgusting. Other vices can be concealed and cherished in secret; anger shows itself openly and appears in the countenance, and the greater it is, the more plainly it boils forth. Do you not see how in all animals certain signs appear before they proceed to mischief, and how their entire bodies put off their usual quiet appearance and stir up their ferocity? Boars foam at the mouth and sharpen their teeth by rubbing them against trees, bulls toss their horns in the air and scatter the sand with blows of their feet, lions growl, the necks of enraged snakes swell, mad dogs have a sullen look — there is no animal so hateful and venomous by nature that it does not, when seized by anger, show additional fierceness. I know well that the other passions, can hardly be concealed, and that lust, fear, and boldness give signs of their presence and may be discovered beforehand, for there is no one of the. stronger passions that does not affect the countenance: what then is the difference between them and anger? Why, that the other passions are visible, but that this is conspicuous.

II.
Next, if you choose to view its results and the mischief that it does, no plague has cost the human race more dear: you will see slaughterings and poisonings, accusations and counter-accusations, sacking of cities, ruin of whole peoples, the persons of princes sold into slavery by auction, torches applied to roofs, and fires not merely confined within city-walls but making whole tracts of country glow with hostile flame. See the foundations of the most celebrated cities hardly now to be discerned; they were ruined by anger. See deserts extending for many miles without an inhabitant: they have been desolated by anger. See all the chiefs whom tradition mentions as instances of ill fate; anger stabbed one of them in his bed, struck down another, though he was protected by the sacred rights of hospitality, tore another to pieces in the very home of the laws and in sight of the crowded forum, bade one shed his own blood by the

parricide hand of his son, another to have his royal throat cut by the hand of a slave, another to stretch out his limbs on the cross: and hitherto I am speaking merely of individual cases. What, if you were to pass from the consideration of those single men against whom anger has broken out to view whole assemblies cut down by the sword, the people butchered by the soldiery let loose upon it, and whole nations condemned to death in one common ruin . ..." as though by men who either freed themselves from our charge or despised our authority? Why, wherefore is the people angry with gladiators, and so unjust as to think itself wronged if they do not die cheerfully? It thinks itself scorned, and by looks, gestures, and excitement turns itself from a mere spectator into an adversary. Everything of this sort is not anger, but the semblance of anger, like that of boys who want to beat the ground when they have fallen upon it, and who often do not even know why they are angry, but are merely angry without any reason or having received any injury, yet not without some semblance of injury received, or without some wish to exact a penalty for it. Thus they are deceived by the likeness of blows, and are appeased by the pretended tears of those who deprecate their wrath, and thus an unreal grief is healed by an unreal revenge.

III.

"We often are angry," says our adversary, "not with men who have hurt us, but with men who are going to hurt us: so you may be sure that anger is not born of injury." It is true that we are angry with those who are going to hurt us, but they do already hurt us in intention, and one who is going to do an injury is already doing it. "The weakest of men," argues he, " are often angry with the most powerful: so you may be sure that anger is not a desire to punish their antagonist — for men do not desire to punish him when they cannot hope to do so." In the first place, I spoke of a desire to inflict punishment, not a power to do so: now men desire even what they cannot obtain. In the next place, no one is so low in station as not to be able to hope to inflict punishment even upon the greatest of men: we all are powerful for mischief. Aristotle's definition differs little from mine: for he declares anger to be a desire to repay suffering. It would be a long task to examine the differences between his definition and mine: it may be urged against both of them that wild beasts become angry without being excited by injury, and without any idea of punishing others or requiting them with pain: for, even though they do these things, these are not what they aim at doing. We must admit, however, that neither wild beasts nor any other creature except man is subject to anger: for, whilst anger is the foe of reason, it nevertheless does not arise in any place where reason cannot dwell. Wild beasts have impulses, fury, cruelty, combativeness : they have not anger any more than they have luxury: yet they indulge in some pleasures with less self-control than human beings. Do not believe the poet who says:

"The boar his wrath forgets, the stag forgets the hounds,
The bear forgets how 'midst the herd he leaped with frantic bounds."
When he speaks of beasts being angry he means that they are excited, roused up: for indeed they know no more how to be angry than they know how to pardon. Dumb creatures have not human feelings, but have certain impulses which resemble them: for if it were not so, if they could feel love and hate, they would likewise be capable of friendship and enmity, of disagreement and agreement. Some traces of these qualities exist even in them, though properly all of them, whether good or bad, belong to the human breast alone. To no creature besides man has been given wisdom, foresight, industry, and reflexion. To animals not only human virtues but even human vices are forbidden: their whole constitution, mental and bodily, is unlike that of human beings: in them the royal and

leading principle is drawn from another source, as, for instance, they possess a voice, yet not a clear one, but indistinct and incapable of forming words: a tongue, but one which is fettered and not sufficiently nimble for complex movements: so, too, they possess intellect, the greatest attribute of all, but in a rough and inexact condition. It is, consequently, able to grasp those visions and semblances which rouse it to action, but only in a cloudy and indistinct fashion. It follows from this that their impulses and outbreaks are violent, and that they do not feel fear, anxieties, grief, or anger, but some semblances of these feelings: wherefore they quickly drop them and adopt the converse of them: they graze after showing the most vehement rage and terror, and after frantic bellowing and plunging they straightway sink into quiet sleep.

IV.
What anger is has been sufficiently explained. The difference between it and irascibility is evident: it is the same as that between a drunken man and a drunkard; between a frightened man and a coward. It is possible for an angry man not to be irascible ; an irascible man may sometimes not be angry. I shall omit the other varieties of anger, which the Greeks distinguish by various names, because we have no distinctive words for them in our language,

although we call men bitter and harsh, and also peevish, frantic, clamorous, surly and fierce: all of which are different forms of irascibility. Among these you may class sulkiness, a refined form of irascibility; for there are some sorts of anger which go no further than noise, while some are as lasting as they are common: some are fierce in deed, but inclined to be sparing of words: some expend themselves in bitter words and curses: some do not go beyond complaining and turning one's back: some are great, deep-seated, and brood within a man: there are a thousand other forms of a multiform evil.

V.
We have now finished our enquiry as to what anger is, whether it exists in any other creature besides man, what the difference is between it and irascibility, and how many forms it possesses. Let us now enquire whether anger be in accordance with nature, and whether it be useful and worth entertaining in some measure.

Whether it be according to nature will become evident if we consider man's nature, than which what is more gentle while it is in its proper condition? Yet what is more cruel than anger? What is more affectionate to others than man? Yet what is more savage against them than anger?

Mankind is born for mutual assistance, anger for mutual ruin: the former loves society, the latter estrangement. The one loves to do good, the other to do harm ; the one to help even strangers, the other to attack even its dearest friends. The one is ready even to sacrifice itself for the good of others, the other to plunge into peril provided it drags others with it. Who, then, can be more ignorant of nature than he who classes this cruel and hurtful vice as belonging to her best and most polished work? Anger, as we have said, is eager to punish; and that such a desire should exist in man's peaceful breast is least of all according to his nature; for human life is founded on brnefits and harmony and is bound together into an alliance for the common help of all, not by terror, but by love towards one another.

VI.

"What, then? Is not correction sometimes necessary?" Of course it is; but with discretion, not with anger; for it does not injure, but heals under the guise of injury. We char crooked spearshafts to straighten them, and force them by driving in wedges, not in order to break them, but to take the bends out of them; and, in like manner, by applying pain to the body or mind we correct dispositions which have been rendered crooked by vice. So the physician at first, when dealing with slight disorders, tries not to make much change in his patient's daily habits, to regulate his food, drink, and exercise, and to improve his health merely by altering the order in which he tikes them. The next step is to see whether an alteration in their amount will be of service. If neither alteration of the order or of the amount is of use, he cuts off some and reduces others. If even this does not answer, he forbids food, and disburdens the body by fasting. If milder remedies have proved useless he opens a vein; if the extremities are injuring the body and infecting it with disease he lays his hands upon the limbs; yet none of his treatment is considered harsh if its result is to give health. Similarly, it is the duty of the chief administrator of the laws, or the ruler of a state, to correct ill-disposed men, as long as he is able, with words, and even with gentle ones, that he may persuade them to do what they ought, inspire them with a love of honour and justice, and cause them to hate vice and set store upon virtue. He must then pass on to severer language, still confining himself to advising and reprimanding; last of all he must betake himself to punishments, yet still making them slight and temporary. He ought to assign extreme punishments only to extreme crimes, that no one may die unless it be even to the criminal's own advantage that he should die. He will differ from the physician in one point alone; for whereas physicians render it easy to die for those to whom they cannot grant the boon of life, he will drive the condemned out of life with ignominy and disgrace, not because he takes pleasure in any man's being punished, for the wise man is far from such inhuman ferocity, but that they may be a warning to all men, and that, since they would not be useful when alive, the state may at any rate profit by their death. Man's nature is not, therefore, desirous of inflicting punishment; neither, therefore, is anger in accordance with man's nature, because that is desirous of inflicting punishment. I will also adduce Plato's argument—for what harm is there in using other men's arguments, so far as they are on our side? "A good man," says he, "does not do any hurt: it is only punishment which hurts. Punishment, therefore, does not accord with a good man: wherefore anger does not do so either, because punishment and anger accord one with another. If a good man takes no pleasure in punishment, he will also take no pleasure in that state of mind to which punishment gives pleasure: consequently anger is not natural to man."

VII.
May it not be that, although anger be not natural, it may be right to adopt it, because it often proves useful? It rouses the spirit and

excites it; and courage does nothing grand in war without it, unless its flame be supplied from this source; this is the goad which stirs up bold men and sends them to encounter perils. Some therefore consider it to be best to control anger, not to banish it utterly, but to cut off its extravagances, and force it to keep within useful bounds, so as to retain that part of it without which action will become languid and all strength and activity of mind will die away.

In the first place, it is easier to banish dangerous passions than to rule them; it is easier not to admit them than to keep them in order when admitted; for when they have established themselves in possession of the mind they are more powerful than the lawful ruler, and will in no wise permit themselves to be weakened or abridged. In the next place, Reason herself, who holds the reins, is only strong while she remains apart from the passions; if she mixes and befouls herself with them she becomes no longer able to restrain those whom she might once have cleared out of her path; for the mind, when once excited and shaken up, goes whither the passions drive it. There are certain things whose beginnings lie in our own power, but which, when developed, drag us along by their own force and leave us no retreat. Those who have flung themselves over a precipice have no control over their movements, nor can they stop or slacken their pace when once started, for their own headlong and irremediable rashness has left no room for either reflexion or remorse, and they cannot help going to lengths which they might have avoided. So, also, the mind, when it has abandoned itself to anger, love, or any other passion, is unable to check itself: its own weight and the downward tendency of vices must needs carry the man off and hurl him into the lowest depth.

VIII.
The best plan is to reject straightway the first incentives to anger, to resist its very beginnings, and to take care not to be betrayed into it: for if once it begins to carry us away, it is hard to get back again into a healthy condition, because reason goes for nothing when once passion has been admitted to the mind, and has by our own free will been given a certain authority, it will for the future do as much as it chooses, not only as much as you will allow it. The enemy, I repeat, must be met and driven back at the outermost frontier-line: for when he has once entered the city and passed its gates, he will not allow his prisoners to set bounds to his victory. The mind does not stand apart and view its passions from without, so as not to permit them to advance further than they ought, but it is itself changed into

a passion, and is therefore unable to check what once was useful and wholesome strength, now that it has become degenerate and misapplied: for passion and reason, as I said before, have not distinct and separate provinces, but consist of the changes of the mind itself for better or for worse. How then can reason recover itself when it is conquered and held down by vices, when it has given way to anger? or how can it extricate itself from a confused mixture, the greater part of which consists of the lower qualities ? "But," argues our adversary, "some men when in anger control themselves." Do they so far control themselves that they do nothing which anger dictates, or somewhat? If they do nothing thereof, it becomes evident that anger is not essential to the conduct of affairs, although your sect advocated it as possessing greater strength than reason Finally, I ask, is anger stronger or weaker than reason? If stronger, how can reason impose any check upon it, since it is only the less powerful that obey: if weaker, then reason is competent to effect its ends without anger, and does not need the help of a less powerful quality. "But some angry men remain consistent and control themselves." When do they do so? It is when their anger is disappearing and leaving them of its own accord, not when it was red-hot, for then it was more powerful than they. "What then? do not men, even in the height of their anger, sometimes let their enemies go whole and unhurt, and refrain from injuring them?" They do: but when do they do so? It is when one passion overpowers another, and either fear or greed gets the upper hand for a while. On such occasions, it is not thanks to reason that anger is stilled, but owing to an untrustworthy and fleeting truce between the passions.

IX.
In the next place, anger has nothing useful in itself, and does not rouse up the mind to warlike deeds: for a virtue, being self-sufficient, never needs the assistance of a vice: whenever it needs an impetuous effort, it does not become angry, but rises to the occasion, and excites or soothes itself as far as it deems requisite, just as the machines which hurl darts may be twisted to a greater or lesser degree of tension at the manager's pleasure. "Anger," says Aristotle, "is necessary, nor can any fight be won without it, unless it fills the mind, and kindles up the spirit. It must, however, be made use of, not as a general, but as a soldier." Now this is untrue; for if it listens to reason and follows whither reason leads, it is no longer anger, whose characteristic is obstinacy: if, again, it is disobedient and will not be quiet when ordered, but is carried

away by its own willful and headstrong spirit, it is then as useless an aid to the mind as a soldier who disregards the sounding of the retreat would be to a general. If, therefore, anger allows limits to be imposed upon it, it must be called by some other name, and ceases to be anger, which I understand to be unbridled and unmanageable: and if it does not allow limits to be imposed upon it, it is harmful and not to be counted among aids: wherefore either anger is not anger, or it is useless: for if any man demands the infliction of punishment, not because he is eager for the punishment itself, but because it is right to inflict it, he ought not to be counted as an angry man: that will be the useful soldier, who knows how to obey orders: the passions cannot obey any more than they can command.

X.
For this cause reason will never call to its aid blind and fierce impulses, over whom she herself possesses no authority, and which she never can restrain save by setting against them similar and equally powerful passions, as for example, fear against anger, anger against sloth, greed against timidity. May virtue never come to such a pass, that reason should fly for aid to vices! The mind can find no safe repose there, it must needs be shaken and tempest-tossed if it be safe only because of its own defects,

if it cannot be brave without anger, diligent without greed, quiet without fear: such is the despotism under which a man must live if he becomes the slave of a passion. Are you not ashamed to put virtues under the patronage of vices? Then, too, reason ceases to have any power if she can do nothing without passion, and begins to be equal and like unto passion; for what difference is there between them if passion without reason be as rash as reason without passion is helpless? They are both on the same level, if one cannot exist without the other. Yet who could endure that passion should be made equal to reason? "Then," says our adversary, "passion is useful, provided it be moderate." Nay, only if it be useful by nature: but if it be disobedient to authority and reason, all that we gain by its moderation is that the less there is of it, the less harm it does: wherefore a moderate passion is nothing but a moderate evil.

XI.
"But," argues he, "against our enemies anger is necessary." In no case is it less necessary; since our attacks ought not to be disorderly, but regulated and under control. What, indeed, is it except anger, so ruinous to itself, that overthrows barbarians, who have so much more bodily strength than we, and are so much better able to endure fatigue? Gladiators, too, protect

themselves by skill, but expose themselves to wounds when they are angry. Moreover, of what use is anger, when the same end can be arrived at by reason? Do you suppose that a hunter is angry with the beasts he kills? Yet he meets them when they attack him, and follows them when they flee from him, all of which is managed by reason without anger. When so many thousands of Cimbri and Teutones poured over the Alps, what was it that caused them to perish so completely, that no messenger, only common rumour, carried the news of that great defeat to their homes, except that with them anger stood in the place of courage? and anger, although sometimes it overthrows and breaks to pieces whatever it meets, yet is more often its own destruction. Who can be braver than the Germans? who charge more boldly? who have more love of arms, among which they are born and bred, for which alone they care, to the neglect of everything else? Who can be more hardened to undergo every hardship, since a large part of them have no store of clothing for the body, no shelter from the continual rigour of the climate: yet Spaniards and Gauls, and even the unwarlike races of Asia and Syria cut them down before the main legion comes within sight, nothing but their own irascibility exposing them to death. Give but intelligence to those minds, and discipline to those bodies of theirs, which now are ignorant of vicious refinements, luxury, and wealth, — to say nothing more, we should certainly be obliged to go back to the ancient Roman habits of life. By what did Fabius restore the shattered forces of the state, except by knowing how to delay and spin out time, which angry men know not how to do? The empire, which then was at its last gasp, would have perished if Fabius had been as daring as anger urged him to be: but he took thought about the condition of affairs, and after counting his force, no part of which could be lost without everything being lost with it, he laid aside thoughts of grief and revenge, turning his sole attention to what was profitable and to making the most of his opportunities, and conquered his anger before he conquered Hannibal. What did Scipio do? Did he not leave behind Hannibal and the Carthaginian army, and all with whom he had a right to be angry, and carry over the war into Africa with such deliberation that he made his enemies think him luxurious and lazy? What did the second Scipio do? Did he not remain a long, long time before Numantia, and bear with calmness the reproach to himself and to his country that Numantia took longer to conquer than Carthage? By blockading and investing his enemies, he brought them to such straits that they perished by their own swords. Anger, therefore, is not useful even in wars or battles: for it is prone to rashness, and while trying to bring others into danger, does not guard itself against danger. The most trustworthy virtue is that which long and carefully considers itself, controls itself, and slowly and deliberately brings itself to the front.

XII.
"What, then," asks our adversary, "is a good man not to be angry if he sees his father murdered or his mother outraged?" No, he will not be angry, but will avenge them, or protect them. Why do you fear that filial piety will not prove a sufficient spur to him even without anger? You may as well say — "What then? When a good man sees his father or his son being cut down, I suppose he will not weep or faint," as we see women do whenever any trifling rumour of danger reaches them. The good man will do his duty without disturbance or fear, and he will perform the duty of a good man, so as to do nothing unworthy of a man. My father will be murdered: then I will defend him: he has been slain, then I will avenge him, not because I am grieved, but because it is my duty. "Good men are made angry by injuries done to their friends." When you say this, Theophrastus, you seek to throw discredit upon more manly maxims; you leave the judge and appeal to the mob: because everyone is angry when such things befall

his own friends, you suppose that men will decide that it is their duty to do what they do: for as a rule every man considers a passion which he recognises to be a righteous one. But he does the same thing if the hot water is not ready for his drink, if a glass be broken, or his shoe splashed with mud. It is not filial piety, but weakness of mind that produces this anger, as children weep when they lose their parents, just as they do when they lose their toys. To feel anger on behalf of one's friends does not show a loving, but a weak mind: it is admirable and worthy conduct to stand forth as the defender of one's parents, children, friends, and countrymen, at the call of duty itself, acting of one's own free will, forming a deliberate judgment, and looking forward to the future, not in an impulsive, frenzied fashion. No passion is more eager for revenge than anger, and for that very reason it is unapt to obtain it: being over hasty and frantic, like almost all desires, it hinders itself in the attainment of its own object, and therefore has never been useful either in peace or war: for it makes peace like war, and when in arms forgets that Mars belongs to neither side, and falls into the power of the enemy, because it is not in its own. In the next place, vices ought not to be received into common use because on some occasions they have effected somewhat: for so also fevers are good for certain kinds of ill-health, but nevertheless it is better to be altogether free from them: it is a hateful mode of cure to owe one's health to disease. Similarly, although anger, like poison, or falling headlong, or being shipwrecked, may have unexpectedly done good, yet it ought not on that account to be classed as wholesome, for poisons have often proved good for the health.

XIII.

Moreover, qualities which we ought to possess become better and more desirable the more extensive they are: if justice is a good thing, no one will say that it would be better if any part were subtracted from it; if bravery is a good thing, no one would wish it to be in any way curtailed: consequently the greater anger is, the better it is, for whoever objected to a good thing being increased? But it is not expedient that anger should be increased: therefore it is not expedient that it should exist at all, for that which grows bad by increase cannot be a good thing. "Anger is useful," says our adversary, "because it makes men more ready to fight." According to that mode of reasoning, then, drunkenness also is a good thing, for it makes men insolent and daring, and many use their weapons better when the worse for liquor: nay, according to that reasoning, also, you may call frenzy and madness essential to strength, because madness often makes men stronger. Why, does not fear often by the rule of contraries make men bolder, and does not the terror of death rouse up even arrant cowards to join battle? Yet anger, drunkenness, fear, and the like, are base and temporary incitements to action, and can furnish no arms to virtue, which has no need of vices, although they may at times be of some little assistance to sluggish and cowardly minds. No man becomes braver through anger, except one who without anger would not have been brave at all: anger does not therefore come to assist courage, but to take its place. What are we to say to the argument that, if anger were a good thing it would attach itself to all the best men? Yet the most irascible of creatures are infants, old men, and sick people. Every weakling is naturally prone to complaint.

XIV.

It is impossible, says Theophrastus, for a good man not to be angry with bad men. By this reasoning, the better a man is, the more irascible he will be: yet will he not rather be more tranquil, more free from passions, and hating no one: indeed, what reason has he for hating sinners, since it is error that leads them into such crimes? now it does not become a sensible man to hate the erring, since if so he will hate himself: let him think how many things he does contrary to good morals, how much of what he has done stands in need of pardon, and he will soon become angry with himself also, for no righteous judge pronounces a different judgment in his own case and in that of others. No one, I affirm, will be found who can acquit himself. Every one when he calls himself innocent looks rather to external witnesses than to his own conscience. How much more philanthropic it is to deal with the erring in a gentle and fatherly spirit, and to call them into the right course instead of hunting them down? When a man is wandering about our fields because he has lost his way, it is better to place him on the right path than to drive him away.

XV.

The sinner ought, therefore, to be corrected both by warning and by force, both by gentle and harsh means, and may be made a better man both towards himself and others by chastisement, but not by anger: for who is angry with the patient whose wounds he is tending ? "But they cannot be corrected, and there is nothing in them that is gentle or that admits of good hope." Then let them be removed from mortal society, if they are likely to deprave everyone with whom they come in contact, and let them cease to be bad men in the only way in which they can: yet let this be done without hatred: for what reason have I for hating the man to whom I am doing the greatest good, since I am rescuing him from himself? Does a man hate his own limbs when he cuts them off? That is not an act of anger, but a lamentable method of healing. We knock mad dogs on the head, we slaughter fierce and savage bulls, and we doom scabby sheep to the knife, lest they should infect our flocks: we destroy monstrous births, and we also drown our children if they are born weakly or unnaturally formed; to separate what is useless from what is sound is an act, not of anger, but of reason. Nothing becomes one who inflicts punishment less than anger, because the punishment has all the more power to work reformation if the sentence be pronounced with deliberate judgment. This is why Socrates said to the slave, "I would strike you, were I not angry." He put off the correction of the slave to a calmer season; at the moment, he corrected himself. Who can boast that he has his passions under control, when Socrates did not dare to trust himself to his anger?

XVI.
We do not, therefore, need an angry chastiser to punish the erring and wicked: for since anger is a crime of the mind, it is not right that sins should be punished by sin. "What! am I not to be angry with a robber, or a poisoner?" No: for I am not angry with

myself when I bleed myself. I apply all kinds of punishment as remedies. You are as yet only in the first stage of error, and do not go wrong seriously, although you do so often: then I will try to amend you by a reprimand given first in private and then in public. You, again, have gone too far to be restored to virtue by words alone; you must be kept in order by disgrace. For the next, some stronger measure is required, something that he can feel must be branded upon him; you, sir, shall be sent into exile and to a desert place. The next man's thorough villainy needs harsher remedies: chains and public imprisonment must be applied to him. You, lastly, have an incurably vicious mind, and add crime to crime: you have come to such a pass, that you are not influenced by the arguments which are never wanting to recommend evil, but sin itself is to you a sufficient reason for sinning: you have so steeped your whole heart in wickedness, that wickedness cannot be taken from you without bringing your heart with it. Wretched man! you have long sought to die; we will do you good service, we will take away that madness from which you suffer, and to you who have so long lived a misery to yourself and to others, we will give the only good thing which remains, that is, death. Why should I be angry with a man just when I am doing him good: sometimes the truest form of compassion is to put a man to death. If I were a skilled and learned physician, and were to enter a hospital, or a rich man's house, I should not have prescribed the same treatment for all the patients who were suffering from various diseases. I see different kinds of vice in the vast number of different minds, and am called in to heal the whole body of citizens: let us seek for the remedies proper for each disease. This man may be cured by his own sense of honour, that one by travel, that one by pain, that one by want, that one by the sword. If, therefore, it becomes my duty as a magistrate to put on black robes, and summon an assembly by the sound of a trumpet, I shall walk to the seat of judgment not in a rage or in a hostile spirit, but with the countenance of a judge; I shall pronounce the formal sentence in a grave and gentle rather than a furious voice, and shall bid them proceed sternly, yet not angrily. Even when I command a criminal to be beheaded, when I sew a parricide up in a sack, when I send a man to be punished by military law, when I fling a traitor or public enemy down the Tarpeian Rock, I shall be free from anger, and shall look and feel just as though I were crushing snakes and other venomous creatures. "Anger is necessary to enable us to punish." What? Do you think that the law is angry with men whom it does not know, whom it has never seen, who it hopes will never exist? We ought, therefore, to adopt the law's frame of mind, which does not become angry, but merely defines offences: for, if it is right for a good man to be angry at wicked crimes, it will also be right for him to be moved with envy at the prosperity of wicked men: what, indeed, is more scandalous than that in some cases the very men, for whose deserts no fortune could be found bad enough, should flourish and actually be the spoiled children of success? Yet he will see their affluence without envy, just as he sees their crimes without anger: a good judge condemns wrongful acts, but does not hate them. "What then? when the wise man is dealing with something of this kind, will his mind not be affected by it and become excited beyond its usual wont?" I admit that it will: he will experience a slight and trifling emotion; for, as Zeno says, "Even in the mind of the wise man, a scar remains after the wound is quite healed." He will, therefore, feel certain hints and semblances of passions; but he will be free from the passions themselves.

XVII.
Aristotle says that "certain passions, if one makes a proper use of them, act as arms ": which would be true if, like weapons of war, they could be taken up or laid aside at the pleasure of their wielder. These arms, which Aristotle assigns to virtue, fight of their own accord, do not wait to be seized by the hand, and possess a man instead of being

possessed by him. We have no need of external weapons, nature has equipped us sufficiently by giving us reason. She has bestowed this weapon upon us, which is strong, imperishable, and obedient to our will, not uncertain or capable of being turned against its master. Reason suffices by itself not merely to take thought for the future, but to manage our affairs: what, then, can be more foolish than for reason to beg anger for protection, that is, for what is certain to beg of what is uncertain? what is trustworthy of what is faithless? what is whole of what is sick? What, indeed? since reason is far more powerful by itself even in performing those operations in which the help of anger seems especially needful: for when reason has decided that a particular thing should be done, she perseveres in doing it; not being able to find anything better than herself to exchange with. She, therefore, abides by her purpose when it has once been formed; whereas anger is often overcome by pity: for it possesses no firm strength, but merely swells like an empty bladder, and makes a violent beginning, just like the winds which rise from the earth and are caused by rivers and marshes, which blow furiously without any continuance: anger begins with a mighty rush, and then falls away, becoming fatigued too soon: that which but lately thought of nothing but cruelty and novel forms of torture, is become quite softened and gentle when the time comes for punishment to be inflicted. Passion soon cools, whereas reason is always consistent: yet even in cases where anger has continued to burn, it often happens that although there may be many who deserve to die, yet after the death of two or three it ceases to slay. Its first onset is fierce, just as the teeth of snakes when first roused from their lair are venomous, but become harmless after repeated bites have exhausted their poison. Consequently those who are equally guilty are not equally punished, and often he who has done less is punished more, because he fell in the way of anger when it was fresher. It is altogether irregular; at one time it runs into undue excess, at another it falls short of its duty: for it indulges its own feelings and gives sentence according to its caprices, will not listen to evidence, allows the defence no opportunity of being heard, clings to what it has wrongly assumed, and will not suffer its opinion to be wrested from it, even when it is a mistaken one.

XVIII.
Reason gives each side time to plead; moreover, she herself demands adjournment, that she may have sufficient scope for the discovery of the truth; whereas anger is in a hurry: reason wishes

to give a just decision; anger wishes its decision to be thought just: reason looks no further than the matter in hand; anger is excited by empty matters hovering on the outskirts of the case: it is irritated by anything approaching to a confident demeanour, a loud voice, an unrestrained speech, dainty apparel, high-flown pleading, or popularity with the public. It often condemns a man because it dislikes his patron; it loves and maintains error even when truth is staring it in the face. It hates to be proved wrong, and thinks it more honourable to persevere in a mistaken line of conduct than to retract it. I remember Gnaeus Piso, a man who was free from many vices, yet of a perverse disposition, and one who mistook harshness for consistency. In his anger he ordered a soldier to be led off to execution because he had returned from furlough without his comrade, as though he must have murdered him if he could not show him. When the man asked for time for search, he would not grant it: the condemned man was brought outside the rampart, and was just offering his neck to the axe, when suddenly there appeared his comrade who was thought to be slain. Hereupon the centurion in charge of the execution bade the guardsman sheathe his sword, and led the condemned man back to Piso, to restore to him the innocence which Fortune had restored to the soldier. They were led into his presence by their fellow soldiers amid the great joy of the whole camp, embracing one another and accompanied by a vast crowd. Piso mounted the tribunal in a fury and ordered them both to be executed, both him who had not murdered and him who had not been slain. What could be more unworthy than this? Because one was proved to be innocent, two perished. Piso even added a third: for he actually ordered the centurion, who had brought back the condemned man, to be put to death. Three men were set up to die in the same place because one was innocent. O, how clever is anger at inventing reasons for its frenzy! "You," it says, "I order to be executed, because you have been condemned to death: you, because you have been the cause of your comrade's condemnation, and you, because when ordered to put him to death you disobeyed your general." He discovered the means of charging them with three crimes, because he could find no crime in them.

XIX.
Irascibility, I say, has this fault—it is loath to be ruled: it is angry with the truth itself, if it comes to light against its will: it assails those whom it has marked for its victims with shouting and riotous noise and gesticulation of the entire body, together with reproaches

and curses. Not thus does reason act: but if it must be so, she silently and quietly wipes out whole households, destroys entire families of the enemies of the state, together with their wives and children, throws down their very dwellings, levels them with the ground, and roots out the names of those who are the foes of liberty. This she does without grinding her teeth or shaking her head, or doing anything unbecoming to a judge, whose countenance ought to be especially calm and composed at the time when he is pronouncing an important sentence. "What need is there," asks Hieronymus, "for you to bite your own lips when you want to strike some one?" What would he have said, had he seen a proconsul leap down from the tribunal, snatch the fasces from the lictor, and tear his own clothes because those of others were not torn as fast as he wished. "Why need you upset the table, throw down the drinking cups, knock yourself against the columns, tear your hair, smite your thigh and your breast? How vehement do you suppose anger to be, if it thus turns back upon itself, because it cannot find vent on another as fast as it wishes? Such men, therefore, are held back by the bystanders and are begged to become reconciled with themselves. But he who while free from anger assigns to each man the penalty which he deserves, does none of these things. He often lets a man go after detecting his crime, if his penitence for what he has done gives good hope for the future, if he perceives that the man's wickedness is not deeply rooted in his mind, but is only, as the saying is, skindeep. He will grant impunity in cases where it will hurt neither the receiver nor the giver. In some cases he will punish great crimes more leniently than lesser ones, if the former were the result of momentary impulse, not of cruelty, while the latter were instinct with secret, under-hand, long-practised craftiness. The same fault, committed by two separate men, will not be visited by him with the same penalty, if the one was guilty of it through carelessness, the other with a premeditated intention of doing mischief. In all dealing with crime he will remember that the one form of punishment is meant to make bad men better, and the other to put them out of the way. In either case he will look to the future, not to the past: for, as Plato says, "no wise man punishes any one because he has sinned, but that he may sin no more: for what is past cannot be recalled, but what is to come may be checked." Those, too, whom he wishes to make examples of the ill success of wickedness, he executes publicly, not merely in order that they themselves may die, but that by dying they may deter others from doing likewise. You see how free from any mental disturbance a man ought to be who has to weigh and consider all this, when he deals with a matter which ought to be handled with the utmost care, I mean, the power of life and death. The sword of justice is ill-placed in the hands of an angry man.

XX.

Neither ought it to be believed that anger contributes anything to magnanimity: what it gives is not magnanimity but vain glory. The increase which disease produces in bodies swollen with morbid humours is not healthy growth, but bloated corpulence. All those whose madness raises them above human considerations, believe themselves to be inspired with high and sublime ideas; but there is no solid ground beneath, and what is built without foundation is liable to collapse in ruin. Anger has no ground to stand upon, and does not rise from a firm and enduring foundation, but is a windy, empty quality, as far removed from true magnanimity as foolhardiness from courage, boastfulness from confidence, gloom from austerity, cruelty from strictness. There is, I say, a great difference between a lofty and a proud mind: anger brings about nothing grand or beautiful. On the other hand, to be constantly irritated seems to me to be the part of a languid and unhappy mind, conscious of its own feebleness, like folk with diseased bodies covered with sores, who cry out at the lightest touch. Anger, therefore, is a vice which for the most part affects women and children. "Yet it affects men also." Because many men, too, have womanish or childish intellects. "But what are we to say? do not some words fall from angry men which appear to flow from a great mind?" Yes, to those who know not what true greatness is: as, for example, that foul and hateful saying, " Let them hate me, provided they fear me," which you may be sure was written in Sulla's time. I know not which was the worse of the two things he wished for, that he might be hated or that he might be feared. It occurs to his mind that someday people will curse him, plot against him, crush him: what prayer does he add to this? May all the gods curse him — for discovering a cure for hate so worthy of it. "Let them hate." How? "Provided they obey me?" No!" Provided they approve of me?" No! How then? "Provided they fear me!" I would not even be loved upon such terms. Do you imagine that this was a very spirited saying? You are wrong: this is not greatness, but monstrosity. You should not believe the words of angry men, whose speech is very loud and menacing, while their mind within them is as timid as possible: nor need you suppose that the most eloquent of men, Titus Livius, was right in describing somebody as being "of a great rather than a good disposition." The things cannot be separated: he must either be good or else he cannot be great, because I take greatness of mind to mean that it is unshaken, sound throughout, firm and uniform to its very foundation; such as cannot exist in evil dispositions. Such dispositions may be terrible, frantic, and destructive, but cannot possess greatness; because greatness rests upon goodness, and owes its strength to it. "Yet by speech, action, and all outward show they will make one think them great." True, they will say something which you may think shows a great spirit, like Gaius Caesar, who when angry with heaven because it interfered with his ballet-dancers, whom he imitated more carefully than he attended to them when they acted, and because it frightened his revels by its thunders, surely ill-directed, challenged Jove to fight, and that to the death, shouting the Homeric verse :—

"Carry me off, or I will carry thee!
How great was his madness! He must have believed either that he could not be hurt even by Jupiter himself, or that he could hurt even Jupiter itself. I imagine that this saying of his had no small weight in nerving the minds of the conspirators for their task: for it seemed to be the height of endurance to bear one who could not bear Jupiter.

XXI.

There is therefore nothing great or noble in anger, even when it seems to be powerful and to contemn both gods and men alike. Anyone who thinks that anger produces greatness of mind, would think that luxury produces it: such a man wishes to rest on ivory, to be clothed with purple, and roofed with gold; to remove lands, embank seas, hasten the course of rivers, suspend woods in the air. He would think that avarice shows greatness of mind: for the avaricious man broods over heaps of gold and silver, treats whole provinces as merely fields on his estate, and has larger tracts of country under the charge of single bailiffs than those which consuls once drew lots to administer. He would think that lust shows greatness of mind: for the lustful man swims across straits, castrates troops of boys, and puts himself within reach of the swords of injured husbands with complete scorn of death. Ambition, too, he would think shows greatness of mind: for the ambitious man is not content with office once a year, but, if possible, would fill the calendar of dignities with his name alone, and cover the whole world with his titles. It matters nothing to what heights or lengths these passions may proceed: they are narrow, pitiable, grovelling. Virtue alone is lofty and sublime, nor is anything great which is not at the same time tranquil.

Footnotes

Here a leaf or more has been lost, including the fragment cited in Lactantius, De ira dei, 17 Ira est cupiditas, &c. The entire passage is: — "But the Stoics did not perceive that there is a difference between right and wrong; that there is just and unjust anger: and as they could find no remedy for it, they wished to extirpate it. The Peripatetics, on the other hand, declared that it ought not to be destroyed, but restrained. These I have sufficiently answered in the sixth book of my Institutiones. It is clear that the philosophers did not comprehend the reason of anger, from the definitions of it which Seneca has enumerated in the books 'On Anger' which he has written. 'Anger,' he says, 'is the desire of avenging an injury.' Others, as Posidonius says, call it 'a desire to punish one by whom you think that you have been unjustly injured.' Some have defined it thus, 'Anger is an impulse of the mind to injure him who either has injured you or has sought to injure you.' Aristotle's definition differs but little from our own. He says, 'that anger is a desire to repay suffering,'" etc.

Ovid, "Met." vii. 545-6.

τό ἡγεμονικόν of the Stoics.

The gospel rule, Matt, xviii. 15.

Divitis (where there might be an army of slaves).

"Lorsque le Preteur devoit prononcer la sentence d'un coupable, il se depouilloit de la robe pretexte, et se revètoit alors d'une simple tunique, ou d'une autre robe, presque usee, et d'un blanc sale (sordida) ou d'un gris très foncé tirant sur le noir (toga pulla), telle qu'en portoient à Rome le peuple et les pauvres (pullaque paupertas). Dans les jours solemnelles et marqués par un deuil public, les Senateurs quittoient le laticlave, et les Magistrats la pretexte. La pourpre, la hache, les faisceaux, aucun de ces signes extérieurs de leur dignité ne les distinguoient alors des autres citoyens: sine insignibus Magistratus. Mais ce n'étoit pas seulement pendant le temps ou la ville était plongée dans le deuil et dans l'affliction, que les magistrats s'habilloient comme le peuple (sordidam vestem induebant); ils en usoient de même lorsqu'ils devoient condamner à mort un citoyen. C'est dans ces tristes circonstances qu'ils quittoient la prétexte et prenoient la robe de deuil: perversam vestem. (No doubt "inside out."—J. E. B. M.) "On pourrait supposer avec assez de vraisemblance que par cette expression, Séneque a voulu faire allusion à ce changement...... Peut-être les Magistrats qui devoient juger à mort un citoyen, portoient ils aussi leur robe renversée, ou la jettoient ils de travers ou confusément sur leurs épaules, pour mieux peindre par ce desordre le trouble de leur esprit. Si cette conjecture est vraie, comme je serais assez porté à croire, l'expression perversa vestis, dont Séneque s'est servi ici, indiqueroit plus d'un simple changement d'habit," &c. (La Grange's translation of Seneca, edited by J. A. Naigeon. Paris, 1778.)

"Ceci fait allusion à une coutume que Caius Gracchus prétend avoir été pratiquée de tout tems à Rome. 'Lorsqu'un citoyen,'" dit il, "avoit un procès criminel qui alloit à la mort, s'il refusoit d'obéir aux sommations qui lui étoient faites; le jour qu'on devoit le juger, en envoyoit des le matin à la porte de sa maison un Officier l'appeller au son de la trompette, et jamais avant que cette cérémonie eût été observée, les Juges ne donneroient leur voix contre lui: tant ces hommes sages,' ajoute ce hardi Tribun, 'avoient de retenue et de precaution dans leurs jugements, quand il s'agissoit de la vie d'un citoyen.'" "C'étoit de même au son de la trompette que l'on convoquoit le peuple, lorsqu'on devoit faire mourir un citoyen, afin qu'il fût témoin de ce triste spectacle, et que la supplice du coupable pût lui servir d'exemple. Tacite dit qu'un Astrologue, nommé P. Marcius, fût exécuté, selon l'ancien usage, hors de la porte Esquiline, en presence du peuple Romain que les Consuls firent convoquer au son de la trompette. (Tac. Ann. II. 32.) L. Grom.

i.e., not only for counsel, but for action

Prorsus parum certis

BOOK 2

MY first book, Novatus, had a more abundant subject: for carriages roll easily down hill: now we must proceed to drier matters. The question before us is whether anger arises from deliberate choice or from impulse, that is, whether it acts of its own accord or like the greater part of those passions which spring up within us without our knowledge. It is necessary for our debate to stoop to the consideration of these matters, in order that it may afterwards be able to rise to loftier themes; for likewise in our bodies the parts which are first set in order are the bones, sinews, and joints, which are by no means fair to see, albeit they are the foundation of our frame and essential to its life: next to them come the parts of which all beauty of face and appearance consists; and after these, colour, which above all else charms the eye, is applied last of all, when the rest of the body is complete. There is no doubt that anger is roused by the appearance of an injury being done: but the question before us is, whether anger straightway follows the appearance, and springs up without assistance from the mind, or whether it is roused with the sympathy of the mind. Our (the Stoics') opinion is, that anger can venture upon nothing by itself, without the approval of mind: for to conceive the idea of a wrong having been done, to long to avenge it, and to join the two propositions, that we ought not to have been injured and that it is our duty to avenge our injuries, cannot belong to a mere impulse which is excited without our consent. That impulse is a simple act; this is a complex one, and composed of several parts. The man understands something to have happened: he becomes indignant thereat: he condemns the deed; and he avenges it. All these things cannot be done without his mind agreeing to those matters which touched him.

II.
Whither, say you, does this inquiry tend? That we may know what anger is: for if it springs up against our will, it never will yield to reason: because all the motions which take place without our volition are beyond our control and unavoidable, such as shivering when cold water is poured over us, or shrinking when we are touched in certain places. Men's hair rises up at bad news, their faces blush at indecent words, and they are seized with dizziness when looking down a precipice; and as it is not in our power to prevent any of these things, no reasoning can prevent their taking place. But anger can be put to flight by wise maxims; for it is a voluntary defect of the mind, and not one of those things which are

evolved by the conditions of human life, and which, therefore, may happen even to the wisest of us. Among these and in the first place must be ranked that thrill of the mind which seizes us at the thought of wrongdoing. We feel this even when witnessing the mimic scenes of the stage, or when reading about things that happened long ago. We often feel angry with Clodius for banishing Cicero, and with Antonius for murdering him. Who is not indignant with the wars of Marius, the proscriptions of Sulla? who is not enraged against Theodotus and Achillas and the boy king who dared to commit a more than boyish crime? Sometimes songs excite us, and quickened rhythm and the martial noise of trumpets; so, too, shocking pictures and the dreadful sight of tortures, however well deserved, affect our minds. Hence it is that we smile when others are smiling, that a crowd of mourners makes us sad, and that we take a glowing interest in another's battles; all of which feelings are not anger, any more than that which clouds our brow at the sight of a stage shipwreck is sadness, or what we feel, when we read how Hannibal after Cannae beset the walls of Rome, can be called fear. All these are emotions of minds which are loath to be moved, and are not passions, but rudiments which may grow into passions. So, too, a soldier starts at the sound of a trumpet, although he may be dressed as a civilian and in the midst of a profound peace, and camp horses prick up their ears at the clash of arms. It is said that Alexander, when Xenophantus was singing, laid his hand upon his weapons.

III.
None of these things which casually influence the mind deserve to be called passions: the mind, if I may so express it, rather suffers passions to act upon itself than forms them. A passion, therefore, consists not in being affected by the sights which are presented to us, but in giving way to our feelings and following up these chance promptings: for whoever imagines that paleness, bursting into tears, lustful feelings, deep sighs, sudden flashes of the eyes, and so forth, are signs of passion and betray the state of the mind, is mistaken, and does not understand that these are merely impulses of the body. Consequently, the bravest of men often turns pale while he is putting on his armour; when the signal for battle is given, the knees of the boldest soldier shake for a moment; the heart even of a great general leaps into his mouth just before the lines clash together, and the hands and feet even of the most eloquent orator grow stiff and cold while he is preparing to begin his speech. Anger must not merely move, but break out of bounds,

being an impulse: now, no impulse can take place without the consent of the mind: for it cannot be that we should deal with revenge and punishment without the mind being cognisant of them. A man may think himself injured, may wish to avenge his wrongs, and then may be persuaded by some reason or other to give up his intention and calm down: I do not call that anger, it is an emotion of the mind which is under the control of reason. Anger is that which goes beyond reason and carries her away with it: wherefore the first confusion of a man's mind when struck by what seems an injury is no more anger than the apparent injury itself: it is the subsequent mad rush, which not only receives the impression of the apparent injury, but acts upon it as true, that is anger, being an exciting of the mind to revenge, which proceeds from choice and deliberate resolve. There never has been any doubt that fear produces flight, and anger a rush forward; consider, therefore, whether you suppose that anything can be either sought or avoided without the participation of the mind.

IV.

Furthermore, that you may know in what manner passions begin and swell and gain spirit, learn that the first emotion is involuntary, and is, as it were, a preparation for a passion, and a threatening of one. The next is combined with a wish, though not an obstinate one, as, for example, "It is my duty to avenge myself, because I have been injured," or "It is right that this man should be punished, because he has committed a crime." The third emotion is already beyond our control, because it overrides reason, and wishes to avenge itself, not if it be its duty, but whether or no. We are not able by means of reason to escape from that first impression on the mind, any more than we can escape from those things which we have mentioned as occurring to the body: we cannot prevent other people's yawns temping us to yawn: we cannot help winking when fingers are suddenly darted at our eyes. Reason is unable to overcome these habits, which perhaps might be weakened by practice and constant watchfulness: they differ from an emotion which is brought into existence and brought to an end by a deliberate mental act.

V.
We must also enquire whether those whose cruelty knows no bounds, and who delight in shedding human blood, are angry when they kill people from whom they have received no injury, and who they themselves do not think have done them any injury; such as were Apollodorus or Phalaris. This is not anger, it is ferocity: for it does not do hurt because it has received

injury: but is even willing to receive injury, provided it may do hurt. It does not long to inflict stripes and mangle bodies to avenge its wrongs, but for its own pleasure. What then are we to say? This evil takes its rise from anger; for anger, after it has by long use and indulgence made a man forget mercy, and driven all feelings of human fellowship from his mind, passes finally into cruelty. Such men therefore laugh, rejoice, enjoy themselves greatly, and are as unlike as possible in countenance to angry men, since cruelty is their relaxation. It is said that when Hannibal saw a trench full of human blood, he exclaimed, "O, what a beauteous sight!" How much more beautiful would he have thought it, if it had filled a river or a lake? Why should we wonder that you should be charmed with this sight above all others, you who were born in bloodshed and brought up amid slaughter from a child? Fortune will follow you and favour your cruelty for twenty years, and will display to you everywhere the sight that you love. You will behold it both at Trasumene and at Cannae, and lastly at your own city of Carthage. Volesus, who not long ago, under the Emperor Augustus, was proconsul of Asia Minor, after he had one day beheaded three hundred persons, strutted out among the corpses with a haughty air, as though he had performed some grand and notable exploit, and exclaimed in Greek, "What a kingly action!" What would this man have done, had he been really a king? This was not anger, but a greater and an incurable disease.

VI.
"Virtue," argues our adversary, "ought to be angry with what is base, just as she approves of what is honourable." What should we think if he said that virtue ought to be both mean and great; yet this is what he means, when he wants her to be raised and lowered, because joy at a good action is grand and glorious, while anger at another's sin is base and befits a narrow mind: and virtue will never be guilty of imitating vice while she is repressing it; she considers anger to deserve punishment for itself, since it often is even more criminal than the faults with which it is angry. To rejoice and be glad is the proper and natural function of virtue: it is as much beneath her dignity to be angry, as to mourn: now, sorrow is the companion of anger, and all anger ends in sorrow, either from remorse or from failure. Secondly, if it be the part of the wise man to be angry with sins, he will be more angry the greater they are, and will often be angry: from which it follows that the wise man will not only be angry but irascible. Yet if we do not believe that great and frequent anger can find any place in the wise man's mind, why should we not set

him altogether free from this passion? for there can be no limit, if he ought to be angry in proportion to what every man does: because he will either be unjust if he is equally angry at unequal crimes, or he will be the most irascible of men, if he blazes into wrath as often as crimes deserve his anger.

VII.
What, too, can be more unworthy of the wise man, than that his passions should depend upon the wickedness of others? If so, the great Socrates will no longer be able to return home with the same expression of countenance with which he set out. Moreover, if it be the duty of the wise man to be angry at base deeds, and to be excited and saddened at crimes, then is there nothing more unhappy than the wise man, for all his life will be spent in anger and grief. What moment will there be at which he will not see something deserving of blame? whenever he leaves his house, he will be obliged to walk among men who are criminals, misers, spendthrifts, profligates, and who are happy in being so: he can turn his eyes in no direction without their finding something to shock them. He will faint, if he demands anger from himself as often as reason calls for it. All these thousands who are hurrying to the law courts at break of day, how base are their causes, and how

much baser their advocates? One impugns his father's will, when he would have done better to deserve it; another appears as the accuser of his mother; a third comes to inform against a man for committing the very crime of which he himself is yet more notoriously guilty. The judge, too, is chosen to condemn men for doing what he himself has done, and the audience takes the wrong side, led astray by the fine voice of the pleader.

VIII.
Why need I dwell upon individual cases? Be assured, when you see the Forum crowded with a multitude, the Saepta swarming with people, or the great Circus, in which the greater part of the people find room to show themselves at once, that among them there are as many vices as there are men. Among those whom you see in the garb of peace there is no peace: for a small profit any one of them will attempt the ruin of another: no one can gain anything save by another's loss. They hate the fortunate and despise the unfortunate: they grudgingly endure the great, and oppress the small: they are fired by diverse lusts: they would wreck everything for the sake of a little pleasure or plunder: they live as though they were in a school of gladiators, fighting with the same people with whom they live: it is like a society of wild beasts, save that

beasts are tame with one another, and refrain from biting their own species, whereas men tear one another, and gorge themselves upon one another. They differ from dumb animals in this alone, that the latter are tame with those who feed them, whereas the rage of the former preys on those very persons by whom they were brought up.

IX.
The wise man will never cease to be angry, if he once begins, so full is every place of vices and crimes. More evil is done than can be healed by punishment: men seem engaged in a vast race of wickedness. Every day there is greater eagerness to sin, less modesty. Throwing aside all reverence for what is better and more just, lust rushes whithersoever it thinks fit, and crimes are no longer committed by stealth, they take place before our eyes, and wickedness has become so general and gained such a footing in everyone's breast that innocence is no longer rare, but no longer exists. Do men break the law singly, or a few at a time? Nay, they rise in all quarters at once, as though obeying some universal signal, to wipe out the boundaries of right and wrong.

"Host is not safe from guest,
Father-in-law from son; but seldom love
Exists 'twixt brothers; wives long to destroy

Their husbands, husbands long to slay their wives,
Stepmothers deadly aconite prepare
And child-heirs wonder when their sires will die."

And how small a part of men's crimes are these! The poet has not described one people divided into two hostile camps, parents and children enrolled on opposite sides, Rome set on fire by the hand of a Roman, troops of fierce horsemen scouring the country to track out the hiding- places of the proscribed, wells defiled with poison, plagues created by human .hands, trenches dug by children round their beleaguered parents, crowded prisons, conflagrations that consume whole cities, gloomy tyrannies, secret plots to establish despotisms and ruin peoples, and men glorying in those deeds which, as long as it was possible to repress them, were counted as crimes — I mean rape, debauchery, and lust ...... Add to these, public acts of national bad faith, broken treaties, everything that cannot defend itself carried off as plunder by the stronger, knaveries, thefts, frauds, and disownings of debt such as three of our present law-courts would not suffice to deal with. If you want the wise man to be as angry as the atrocity of men's crimes requires, he must not merely be angry, but must go mad with rage.

X.

You will rather think that we should not be angry with people's faults; for what shall we say of one who is angry with those who stumble in the dark, or with deaf people who cannot hear his orders, or with children, because they forget their duty and interest themselves in the games and silly jokes of their companions? What shall we say if you choose to be angry with weaklings for being sick, for growing old, or becoming fatigued? Among the other misfortunes of humanity is this, that men's intellects are confused, and they not only cannot help going wrong, but love to go wrong. To avoid being angry with individuals, you must pardon the whole mass, you must grant forgiveness to the entire human race. If you are angry with young and old men because they do wrong, you will be angry with infants also, for they soon will do wrong. Does anyone become angry with children, who are too young to comprehend distinctions? Yet, to be a human being is a greater and a better excuse than to be a child. Thus are we born, as creatures liable to as many disorders of the mind as of the body; not dull and slow-witted, but making a bad use of our keenness of wit, and leading one another into vice by our example. He who follows others who have started before him on the wrong road is surely excusable for having wandered on the highway. A general's severity may be shown in the case of individual deserters; but where a whole army deserts, it must needs be pardoned. What is it that puts a stop to the wise man's anger? It is the number of sinners. He perceives how unjust and how dangerous it is to be angry with vices which all men share. Heraclitus, whenever he came out of doors and beheld around him such a number of men who were living wretchedly, nay, rather perishing wretchedly, used to weep: he pitied all those who met him joyous and happy. He was of a gentle but too weak disposition: and he himself was one of those for whom he ought to have wept. Democritus, on the other hand, is said never to have appeared in public without laughing; so little did men's serious occupations appear serious to him. What room is there for anger? Everything ought either to move us to tears or to laughter. The wise man will not be angry with sinners. Why not? Because he knows that no one is born wise, but becomes so: he knows that very few wise men are produced in any age, because he thoroughly understands the circumstances of human life. Now, no sane man is angry with nature: for what should we say if a man chose to be surprised that fruit did not hang on the thickets of a forest, or to wonder at bushes and thorns not being covered with some useful berry? No one is angry when nature excuses a defect. The wise man, therefore, being tranquil, and dealing candidly with mistakes, not an enemy to but an improver of sinners, will go abroad every day in the following frame of mind: — "Many men will meet me who are drunkards, lustful, ungrateful, greedy, and excited by the frenzy of ambition." He will view all these as benignly as a physician does his patients. When a man's ship leaks freely through its opened seams, does he become angry with the sailors or the ship itself? No; instead of that, he tries to remedy it: he shuts out some water, bales out some other, closes all the holes that he can see, and by ceaseless labour counteracts those which are out of sight and which let water into the hold; nor does he relax his efforts because as much water as he pumps out runs in again. We need a long-breathed struggle against permanent and prolific evils; not, indeed, to quell them, but merely to prevent their overpowering us.

XI.
"Anger," says our opponent, "is useful, because it avoids contempt, and because it frightens bad men." Now, in the first place, if anger is strong in proportion to its threats, it is hateful for the same reason that it is terrible: and it is more dangerous to be hated than to be despised. If, again, it is without strength, it is much more exposed

to contempt, and cannot avoid ridicule: for what is more flat than anger when it breaks out into meaningless ravings? Moreover, because some things are somewhat terrible, they are not on that account desirable: nor does wisdom wish itto be said of the wise man, as it is of a wild beast, that the fear which he inspires is as a weapon to him. Why, do we not fear fever, gout, consuming ulcers? and is there, for that reason, any good in them? nay; on the other hand, they are all despised and thought to be foul and base, and are for this very reason feared. So, too, anger is in itself hideous and by no means to be feared; yet it is feared by many, just as a hideous mask is feared by children. How can we answer the fact that terror always works back to him who inspired it, and that no one is feared who is himself at peace? At this point it is well that you should remember that verse of Laberius, which, when pronounced in the theatre during the height of the civil war, caught the fancy of the whole people as though it expressed the national feeling: —

"He must fear many, whom so many fear."
Thus has nature ordained, that whatever becomes great by causing fear to others is not free from fear itself. How disturbed lions are at the faintest noises! How excited those fiercest of beasts become at strange

shadows, voices, or smells! Whatever is a terror to others, fears for itself. There can be no reason, therefore, for any wise man to wish to be feared, and no one need think that anger is anything great because it strikes terror, since even the most despicable things are feared, as, for example, noxious vermin whose bite is venomous: and since a string set with feathers stops the largest herds of wild beasts and guides them into traps, it is no wonder that from its effect it should be named a "Scarer." Foolish creatures are frightened by foolish things: the movement of chariots and the sight of their wheels turning round drives lions back into their cage: elephants are frightened at the cries of pigs: and so also we fear anger just as children fear the dark, or wild beasts fear red feathers: it has in itself nothing solid or valiant, but it affects feeble minds.

XII.
"Wickedness," says our adversary," must be removed from the system of nature, if you wish to remove anger: neither of which things can be done." In the first place, it is possible for a man not to be cold, although according to the system of nature it may be winter-time, nor yet to suffer from heat, although it be summer according to the almanac. He may be protected against the inclement time of the year by dwelling in a

favoured spot, or he may have so trained his body to endurance that it feels neither heat nor cold. Next, reverse this saying: — You must remove anger from your mind before you can take virtue into the same, because vices and virtues cannot combine, and none can at the same time be both an angry man and a good man, any more than he can be both sick and well. "It is not possible," says he, " to remove anger altogether from the mind, nor does human nature admit of it." Yet there is nothing so hard and difficult that the mind of man cannot overcome it, and with which unremitting study will not render him familiar, nor are there any passions so fierce and independent that they cannot be tamed by discipline. The mind can carry out whatever orders it gives itself: some have succeeded in never smiling: some have forbidden themselves wine, sexual intercourse, or even drink of all kinds. Some, who are satisfied with short hours of rest, have learned to watch for long periods without weariness. Men have learned to run upon the thinnest ropes even when slanting, to carry huge burdens, scarcely within the compass of human strength, or to dive to enormous depths and suffer themselves to remain under the sea without any chance of drawing breath. There are a thousand other instances in which application has conquered all obstacles, and proved that nothing which the mind has set itself to endure is difficult. The men whom I have just mentioned gain either no reward or one that is unworthy of their unwearied application; for what great thing does a man gain by applying his intellect to walking upon a tight rope? or to placing great burdens upon his shoulders? or to keeping sleep from his eyes? or to reaching the bottom of the sea? and yet their patient labour brings all these things to pass for a trifling reward. ==Shall not we then call in the aid of patience, we whom such a prize awaits, the unbroken calm of a happy life==? How great a blessing is it to escape from anger, that chief of all evils, and therewith from frenzy, ferocity, cruelty, and madness, its attendants?

XIII.
There is no reason why we should seek to defend such a passion as this or excuse its excesses by declaring it to be either useful or unavoidable. What vice, indeed, is without its defenders ? yet this is no reason why you should declare anger to be ineradicable. The evils from which we suffer are curable, and since we were born with a natural bias towards good, nature herself will help us if we try to amend our lives. Nor is the path to virtue steep and rough, as some think it to be: it may be reached on level ground. This is no untrue tale which I come to tell you: the road to happiness is easy; do you only enter

upon it with good luck and the good help of the gods themselves. It is much harder to do what you are doing. What is more restful than a mind at peace, and what more toilsome than anger? What is more at leisure than clemency, what fuller of business than cruelty? Modesty keeps holiday while vice is overwhelmed with work. In fine, the culture of any of the virtues is easy, while vices require a great expense. Anger ought to be removed from our minds: even those who say that it ought to be kept low admit this to some extent: let it be got rid of altogether; there is nothing to be gained by it. Without it we can more easily and more justly put an end to crime, punish bad men, and amend their lives. The wise man will do his duty in all things without the help of any evil passion, and will use no auxiliaries which require watching narrowly lest they get beyond his control.

XIV.
Anger, then, must never become a habit with us, but we may sometimes affect to be angry when we wish to rouse up the dull minds of those whom we address, just as we rouse up horses who are slow at starting with goads and firebrands. We must sometimes apply fear to persons upon whom reason makes no impression: yet to be angry is of no more use than to grieve or to be afraid. "What? do not circumstances

arise which provoke us to anger?" Yes: but at those times above all others we ought to choke down our wrath. Nor is it difficult to conquer our spirit, seeing that athletes, who devote their whole attention to the basest parts of themselves, nevertheless are able to endure blows and pain, in order to exhaust the strength of the striker, and do not strike when anger bids them, but when opportunity invites them. It is said that Pyrrhus, the most celebrated trainer for gymnastic contests, used habitually to impress upon his pupils not to lose their tempers: for anger spoils their science, and thinks only how it can hurt: so that often reason counsels patience while anger counsels revenge, and we, who might have survived our first misfortunes, are exposed to worse ones. Some have been driven into exile by their impatience of a single contemptuous word, have been plunged into the deepest miseries because they would not endure the most trifling wrong in silence, and have brought upon themselves the yoke of slavery because they were too proud to give up the least part of their entire liberty.

XV.
"That you may be sure," says our opponent, "that anger has in it something noble, pray look at the free nations, such as the Germans and Scythians, who are especially

prone to anger." The reason of this is that stout and daring intellects are liable to anger before they are tamed by discipline; for some passions engraft themselves upon the better class of dispositions only, just as good land, even when waste, grows strong brushwood, and the trees are tall which stand upon a fertile soil. In like manner, dispositions which are naturally bold produce irritability, and, being hot and fiery, have no mean or trivial qualities, but their energy is misdirected, as happens with all those who without training come to the front by their natural advantages alone, whose minds, unless they be brought under control, degenerate from a courageous temper into habits of rashness and reckless daring. "What? are not milder spirits linked with gentler vices, such as tenderness of heart, love, and bashfulness?" Yes, and therefore I can often point out to you a good disposition by its own faults: yet their being the proofs of a superior nature does not prevent their being vices. Moreover, all those nations which are free because they are wild, like lions or wolves, cannot command any more than they can obey: for the strength of their intellect is not civilized, but fierce and unmanageable: now, no one is able to rule unless he is also able to be ruled. Consequently, the empire of the world has almost always remained in the hands of those nations who enjoy a milder climate. Those who dwell near the frozen north have uncivilized temper

"Just on the model of their native skies," as the poet has it.

XVI.
Those animals, urges our opponent, are held to be the most generous who have large capacity for anger. He is mistaken when he holds up creatures who act from impulse instead of reason as patterns for men to follow, because in man reason takes the place of impulse. Yet even with animals, all do not alike profit by the same thing. Anger is of use to lions, timidity to stags, boldness to hawks, flight to doves. What if I declare that it is not even true that the best animals are the most prone to anger? I may suppose that wild beasts, who gain their food by rapine, are better the angrier they are; but I should praise oxen and horses who obey the rein for their patience. What reason, however, have you for referring mankind to such wretched models, when you have the universe and God, whom he alone of animals imitates because he alone comprehends Him ?" The most irritable men," says he, "are thought to be the most straightforward of all." Yes, because they are compared with swindlers and sharpers, and appear to be simple because they are outspoken. I should not call such men

simple, but heedless. We give this title of "simple" to all fools, gluttons, spendthrifts, and men whose vices lie on the surface.

XVII.
"An orator," says our opponent, "sometimes speaks better when he is angry." Not so, but when he pretends to be angry: for so also actors bring down the house by their playing, not when they are really angry, but when they act the angry man well: and in like manner, in addressing a jury or a popular assembly, or in any other position in which the minds of others have to be influenced at our pleasure, we must ourselves pretend to feel anger, fear, or pity before we can make others feel them, and often the pretence of passion will do what the passion itself could not have done. "The mind which does not feel anger," says he, "is feeble." True, if it has nothing stronger than anger to support it. A man ought to be neither robber nor victim, neither tender-hearted nor cruel. The former belongs to an over-weak mind, the latter to an over-hard one. Let the wise man be moderate, and when things have to be done somewhat briskly, let him call force, not anger, to his aid.

XVIII.
Now that we have discussed the questions propounded concerning anger, let us pass on to the consideration of its remedies.

These, I imagine, are two-fold: the one class preventing our becoming angry, the other preventing our doing wrong when we are angry. As with the body we adopt a certain regimen to keep ourselves in health, and use different rules to bring back health when lost, so likewise we must repel anger in one fashion and quench it in another. That we may avoid it, certain general rules of conduct which apply to all men's lives must be impressed upon us. We may divide these into such as are of use during the education of the young and in after-life. Education ought to be carried on with the greatest and most salutary assiduity: for it is easy to mould minds while they are still tender, but it is difficult to uproot vices which have grown up with ourselves.

XIX.
A hot mind is naturally the most prone to anger: for as there are four elements, consisting of fire, air, earth, and water, so there are powers corresponding and equivalent to each of these, namely, hot, cold, dry, and moist. Now the mixture of the elements is the cause of the diversities of lands and of animals, of bodies and of character, and our dispositions incline to one or the other of these according as the strength of each element prevails in us. Hence it is that we call some regions wet or dry, warm or cold. The same distinctions

apply likewise to animals and mankind; it makes a great difference how much moisture or heat a man contains; his character will partake of whichever element has the largest share in him. A warm temper of mind will make men prone to anger; for fire is full of movement and vigour; a mixture of coldness makes men cowards, for cold is sluggish and contracted. Because of this, some of our Stoics think that anger is excited in our breasts by the boiling of the blood round the heart: indeed, that place is assigned to anger for no other reason than because the breast is the warmest part of the whole body. Those who have more moisture in them become angry by slow degrees, because they have no heat ready at hand, but it has to be obtained by movement; wherefore the anger of women and children is sharp rather than strong, and arises on lighter provocation. At dry times of life anger is violent and powerful, yet without increase, and adding little to itself, because as heat dies away cold takes its place. Old men are testy and full of complaints, as also are sick people and convalescents, and all whose store of heat has been consumed by weariness or loss of blood. Those who are wasted by thirst or hunger are in the same condition, as also are those whose frame is naturally bloodless and faints from want of generous diet. Wine kindles anger, because it increases heat; according to each man's disposition, some fly into a passion when they are heavily drunk, some when they are slightly drunk: nor is there any other reason than this why yellow-haired, ruddy-complexioned people should be excessively passionate, seeing that they are naturally of the colour which others put on during anger; for their blood is hot and easily set in motion.

XX.

But just as nature makes some men prone to anger, so there are many other causes which have the same power as nature. Some are brought into this condition by disease or bodily injury, others by hard work, long watching, nights of anxiety, ardent longings, and love: and everything else which is hurtful to the body or the spirit inclines the distempered mind to find fault. All these, however, are but the beginning and causes of anger. Habit of mind has very great power, and, if it be harsh, increases the disorder. As for nature, it is difficult to alter it, nor may we change the mixture of the elements which was formed once for all at our birth: yet knowledge will be so far of service, that we should keep wine out of the reach of hot-tempered men, which Plato thinks ought also to be forbidden to boys, so that fire be not made fiercer. Neither should such men be over-fed: for if so, their bodies will swell, and their minds will swell with them. Such men ought to take exercise, stopping short, however, of fatigue, in order that their natural heat may be abated, but not exhausted, and their excess of fiery spirit may be worked off. Games also will be useful: for moderate pleasure relieves the mind and brings it to a proper balance. With those temperaments which incline to moisture, or dryness and stiffness, there is no danger of anger, but there is fear of greater vices, such as cowardice, moroseness, despair, and suspiciousness: such dispositions therefore ought to be softened, comforted, and restored to cheerfulness: and since we must make use of different remedies for anger and for sullenness, and these two vices require not only unlike, bnt absolutely opposite modes of treatment, let us always attack that one of them which is gaining the mastery.

XXI.
It is, I assure you, of the greatest service to boys that they should be soundly brought up, yet to regulate their education is difficult, because it is our duty to be careful neither to cherish a habit of anger in them, nor to blunt the edge of their spirit. This needs careful watching, for both qualities, both those which are to be encouraged, and those which are to be checked, are fed by the same things; and even a careful

watcher may be deceived by their likeness. A boy's spirit is increased by freedom and depressed by slavery: it rises when praised, and is led to conceive great expectations of itself: yet this same treatment produces arrogance and quickness of temper: we must therefore guide him between these two extremes, using the curb at one time and the spur at another. He must undergo no servile or degrading treatment; he never must beg abjectly for anything, nor must he gain anything by begging; let him rather receive it for his own sake, for his past good behaviour, or for his promises of future good conduct. In contests with his comrades we ought not to allow him to become sulky or fly into a passion: let us see that he be on friendly terms with those whom he contends with, so that in the struggle itself he may learn to wish not to hurt his antagonist but to conquer him: whenever he has gained the day or done something praiseworthy, we should allow him to enjoy his victory, but not to rush into transports of delight: for joy leads to exultation, and exultation leads to swaggering and excessive self-esteem. We ought to allow him some relaxation, yet not yield him up to laziness and sloth, and we ought to keep him far beyond the reach of luxury, for nothing makes children more prone to anger than a soft and fond bringing-up, so that the more only children are indulged, and the more liberty is given to orphans, the more they are corrupted. He to whom nothing is ever denied, will not be able to endure a rebuff, whose anxious mother always wipes away his tears, whose paedagogus is made to pay for his shortcomings. Do you not observe how a man's anger becomes more violent as he rises in station? This shows itself especially in those who are rich and noble, or in great place, when the favouring gale has roused all the most empty and trivial passions of their minds. Prosperity fosters anger, when a man's proud ears are surrounded by a mob of flatterers, saying, "That man answer you! you do not act according to your dignity, you lower yourself." And so forth, with all the language which can hardly be resisted even by healthy and originally well-principled minds. Flattery, then, must be kept well out of the way of children. Let a child hear the truth, and sometimes fear it: let him always reverence it. Let him rise in the presence of his elders. Let him obtain nothing by flying into a passion: let him be given when he is quiet what was refused him when he cried for it: let him behold, but not make use of his father's wealth: let him be reproved for what he does wrong. It will be advantageous to furnish boys with even-tempered teachers and paedagogi: what is soft and unformed clings to what is near, and takes its shape: the habits of young men reproduce those of their nurses and paedagogi. Once, a boy who was brought up in Plato's house went home to his parents, and, on seeing his father shouting with passion, said, "I never saw anyone at Plato's house act like that." I doubt not that he learned to imitate his father sooner than he learned to imitate Plato. Above all, let his food be scanty, his dress not costly, and of the same fashion as that of his comrades: if you begin by putting him on a level with many others, he will not be angry when someone is compared with him.

XXII.

These precepts, however, apply to our children: in ourselves the accident of birth and our education no longer admits of either mistakes or advice; we must deal with what follows. Now we ought to fight against the first causes of evil: the cause of anger is the belief that we are injured; this belief, therefore, should not be lightly entertained. We ought not to fly into a rage even when the injury appears to be open and distinct: for some false things bear the semblance of truth. We should always allow some time- to elapse, for time discloses the truth. Let not our ears be easily lent to calumnious talk: let us know and be on our guard against this fault of human nature, that we are willing to believe what we are unwilling to listen to, and that we become angry before we have formed our opinion. What shall I say? we are influenced not merely by calumnies but by suspicions, and at the very look and smile of others we may fly into a rage with innocent persons because we put the worst construction upon it. We ought, therefore, to plead the cause of the absent against ourselves, and to keep Our anger in abeyance: for a punishment which has been postponed may yet be inflicted, but when once inflicted cannot be recalled.

XXIII.
Everyone knows the story of the tyrannicide who, being caught before he had accomplished his task, and being tortured by Hippias to make him betray his accomplices, named the friends of the tyrant who stood around, and everyone to whom he knew the tyrant's safety was especially dear. As the tyrant ordered each man to be slain as he was named, at last the man, being asked if anyone else remained, said, "You remain alone, for I have left no one else alive to whom you are dear." Anger had made the tyrant lend his assistance to the tyrant-slayer, and cut down his guards with his own sword. How far more spirited was Alexander, who after reading his mother's letter warning him to beware of poison from his physician, Philip, nevertheless drank undismayed the medicine which Philip gave him! He felt

more confidence in his friend: he deserved that his friend should be innocent, and deserved that his conduct should make him innocent. I praise Alexander's doing this all the more because he was above all men prone to anger; but the rarer moderation is among kings, the more it deserves to be praised. The great Gaius Caesar, who proved such a merciful conqueror in the civil war, did the same thing; he burned a packet of letters addressed to Gnaeus Pompeius by persons who had been thought to be either neutrals or on the other side. Though he was never violent in his anger, yet he preferred to put it out of his power to be angry: he thought that the kindest way to pardon each of them was not to know what his offence had been.

XXIV.

Readiness to believe what we hear causes very great mischief; we ought often not even to listen, because in some cases it is better to be deceived than to suspect deceit. We ought to free our minds of suspicion and mistrust, those most untrustworthy causes of anger. "This man's greeting was far from civil; that one would not receive my kiss; one cut short a story I had begun to tell; another did not ask me to dinner; another seemed to view me with aversion." Suspicion will never lack grounds: what we want is straightforwardness, and a kindly interpretation of things. Let us believe nothing unless it forces itself upon bur sight and is unmistakable, and let us reprove ourselves for being too ready to believe, as often as our suspicions prove to be groundless: for this discipline will render us habitually slow to believe what we hear.

XXV.

Another consequence of this will be, that we shall not be exasperated by the slightest and most contemptible trifles. It is mere madness to be put out of temper because a slave is not quick, because the water we are going to drink is lukewarm or because our couch is disarranged or our table carelessly laid. A man must be in a miserably bad state of health if he shrinks from a gentle breath of wind ; his eyes must be diseased if they are distressed by the sight of white clothing; he must be broken down with debauchery if he feels pain at seeing another man work. It is said that there was one Mindyrides, a citizen of Sybaris, who one day seeing a man digging and vigorously brandishing a mattock, complained that the sight made him weary, and forbade the man to work where he could see him. The same man complained that he had suffered from the rose-leaves upon which he lay. being folded double. When pleasures have corrupted both the body and the mind, nothing seems endurable, not indeed because it is hard, but because he who has to bear it is soft: for why should we be driven to frenzy by any one's coughing and sneezing, or by a fly not being driven away with sufficient care, or by a dog's hanging about us, or a key dropping from a careless servant's hand? Will one whose ears are agonised by the noise of a bench being dragged along the floor be able to endure with unruffled mind the rude language of party strife, and the abuse which speakers in the forum or the senate house heap upon their opponents? Will he who is angry with his slave for icing his drink badly, be able to endure hunger, or the thirst of a long march in summer? Nothing, therefore, nourishes anger more than excessive and dissatisfied luxury: the mind ought to be hardened by rough treatment, so as not to feel any blow that is not severe.

XXVI.
We are angry, either with those who can, or with those who cannot do us an injury. To the latter class belong some inanimate things, such as a book, which we often throw away when it is written in letters too small for us to read, or tear up when it is full of mistakes, or clothes which we destroy because we do not like them. How foolish to be angry with such things as these, which neither deserve nor feel our anger! "But of

course it is their makers who really affront us." I answer that, in the first place, we often become angry before making this distinction clear in our minds, and secondly, perhaps even the makers might put forward some reasonable excuses: one of them, it may be, could not make them any better than he did, and it is not through any disrespect to you that he was unskilled in his trade: another may have done his work so without any intention of insulting you: and, finally, what can be more crazy than to discharge upon things the ill-feeling which one has accumulated against persons? Yet as it is the act of a madman to be angry with inanimate objects, so also is it to be angry with dumb animals, which can do us no wrong because they are not able to form a purpose; and we cannot call anything a wrong unless it be done intentionally. They are, therefore, able to hurt us, just as a sword or a stone may do so, but they are not able to do us a wrong. Yet some men think themselves insulted when the same horses which are docile with one rider are restive with another, as though it were through their deliberate choice, and not through habit and cleverness of handling that some horses are more easily managed by some men than by others. And as it is foolish to be angry with them, so it is to be angry with children, and with men who have little more sense than children: for all these sins, before a just judge, ignorance would be as effective an excuse as innocence.

XXVII.
There are some things which are unable to hurt us, and whose power is exclusively beneficial and salutary, as, for example, the immortal gods, who neither wish nor are able to do harm: for their temperament is naturally gentle and tranquil, and no more likely to wrong others than to wrong themselves. Foolish people who know not the truth hold them answerable for storms at sea, excessive rain, and long winters, whereas all the while these phenomena by which we suffer or profit take place without any reference whatever to us: it is not for our sake that the universe causes summer and winter to succeed one another; these have a law of their own, according to which their divine functions are performed. We think too much of ourselves, when we imagine that we are worthy to have such prodigious revolutions effected for our sake: so, then, none of these things take place in order to do us an injury, nay, on the contrary, they all tend to our benefit. I have said that there are some things which cannot hurt us, and some which would not. To the latter class belong good men in authority, good parents, teachers, and judges, whose punishments ought to be submitted to by us in the same spirit in

which we undergo the surgeon's knife, abstinence from food, and such like things which hurt us for our benefit. Suppose that we are being punished; let us think not only of what we suffer, but of what we have done: let us sit in judgement on our past life. Provided we are willing to tell ourselves the truth, we shall certainly decide that our crimes deserve a harder measure than they have received.

XXVIII.
If we desire to be impartial judges of all that takes place, we must first convince ourselves of this, that no one of ns is faultless: for it is from this that most of our indignation proceeds. "I have not sinned, I have done no wrong." Say, rather, you do not admit that you have done any wrong. We are infuriated at being reproved, either by reprimand or actual chastisement, although we are sinning at that very time, by adding insolence and obstinacy to our wrong-doings. Who is there that can declare himself to have broken no laws? Even if there be such a man, what a stinted innocence it is, merely to be innocent by the letter of the law. How much further do the rules of duty extend than those of the law! how many things which are not to be found in the statute book, are demanded by filial feeling, kindness, generosity, equity, and honour? Yet we are not able to warrant

ourselves even to come under that first narrowest definition of innocence: we have done what was wrong, thought what was wrong, wished for what was wrong, and encouraged what was wrong: in some cases we have only remained innocent because we did not succeed. When we think of this, let us deal more justly with sinners, and believe that those who scold us are right: in any case let us not be angry with ourselves (for with whom shall we not be angry, if we are angry even with our own selves ?), and least of all with the gods: for whatever we suffer befalls us not by any ordinance of theirs but of the common law of all flesh. "But diseases and pains attack us." Well, people who live in a crazy dwelling must have some way of escape from it. Someone will be said to have spoken ill of you: think whether you did not first speak ill of him: think of how many persons you have yourself spoken ill. Let us not, I say, suppose that others are doing us a wrong, but are repaying one which we have done them, that some are acting with good intentions, some under compulsion, some in ignorance, and let us believe that even he who does so intentionally and knowingly did not wrong us merely for the sake of wronging us, but was led into doing so by the attraction of saying something witty, or did whatever he did, not out of any spite against us, but because he himself could not succeed unless he pushed us back. We are often offended by flattery even while it is being lavished upon us: yet whoever recalls to his mind how often he himself has been the victim of undeserved suspicion, how often fortune has given his true service an appearance of wrong-doing, how many persons he has begun by hating and ended by loving, will be able to keep himself from becoming angry straightway, especially if he silently says to himself when each offence is committed: "I have done this very thing myself." Where, however, will you find so impartial a judge? The same man who lusts after everyone's wife, and thinks that a woman's belonging to someone else is a sufficient reason for adoring her, will not allow anyone else to look at his own wife. No man expects such exact fidelity as a traitor: the perjurer himself takes vengeance of him who breaks his word : the pettifogging lawyer is most indignant at an action being brought against him: the man who is reckless of his own chastity cannot endure any attempt upon that of his slaves. We have other men's vices before our eyes, and our own behind our backs: hence it is that a father, who is worse than his son, blames the latter for giving extravagant feasts, and disapproves of the least sign of luxury in another, although he was wont to set no bounds to it in his own case; hence it is that despots are angry with homicides, and thefts are punished by those who despoil temples. A great part of mankind is not angry with sins, but with sinners. Regard to our own selves will make us more moderate, if we inquire of ourselves :—have we ever committed any crime of this sort? have we ever fallen into this kind of error? is it for our interest that we should condemn this conduct?

XXIX.

The greatest remedy for anger is delay: beg anger to grant you this at the first, not in order that it may pardon the offence, but that it may form a right judgment about it :- if it delays, it will come to an end. Do not attempt to quell it all at once, for its first impulses are fierce; by plucking away its parts we shall remove the whole. We are made angry by some things which we learn at second-hand, and by some which we ourselves hear or see. Now, we ought to be slow to believe what is told us. Many tell lies in order to deceive us, and many because they are themselves deceived. Some seek to win our favour by false accusations, and invent wrongs in order that they may appear angry at our having suffered them. One man lies out of spite, that he may set trusting friends at variance; some because they are suspicious, and wish to see sport, and watch from a safe distance those whom they have set by the ears. If you were about to give sentence in court about ever so small a sum of money, you would take nothing as proved without a witness, and a witness would count for nothing except on his oath. You would allow both sides to be heard : you would allow them time: you would not despatch the matter at one sitting, because the oftener it is handled the more distinctly the truth appears. And do you condemn your friend offhand? Are you angry with him before you hear his story, before you have cross-examined him, before he can know either who is his accuser or with what he is charged. Why then, just now, in the case which you just tried, did you hear what was said on both sides? This very man who has informed against your friend, will say no more if he be obliged to prove what he says. "You need not," says he, "bring me forward as a witness; if I am brought forward I shall deny what I have said; unless you excuse me from appearing I shall never tell you anything." At the same time he spurs you on and withdraws himself from the strife and battle. The man who will tell you nothing save in secret hardly tells you anything at all. What can be more unjust than to believe in secret, and to be angry openly?

XXX.
Some offences we ourselves witness: in these cases let us examine the disposition

and purpose of the offender. Perhaps he is a child; let us pardon his youth, he knows not whether he is doing wrong: or he is a father; he has either rendered such great services, as to have won the right even to wrong ns—or perhaps this very act which offends ns is his chief merit: or a woman; well, she made a mistake. The man did it because he was ordered to do it. Who but an unjust person can be angry with what is done under compulsion? You had hurt him: well, there is no wrong in suffering the pain which you have been the first to inflict. Suppose that your opponent is a judge; then you ought to take his opinion rather than your own: or that he is a king; then, if he punishes the guilty, yield to him because he is just, and if he punishes the innocent, yield to him because he is powerful. Suppose that it is a dumb animal or as stupid as a dumb animal: then, if you are angry with it, you will make yourself like it. Suppose that it is a disease or a misfortune; it will take less effect upon you if you bear it quietly: or that it is a god; then you waste your time by being angry with him as much as if you prayed him to be angry with someone else. Is it a good man who has wronged you? do not believe it: is it a bad one? do not be surprised at this; he will pay to someone else the penalty which he owes to you—indeed, by his sin he has already punished himself.

XXXI.

There are, as I have stated, two cases which produce anger: first, when we appear to have received an injury, about which enough has been said, and, secondly, when we appear to have been treated unjustly: this must now be discussed. Men think some things unjust because they ought not to suffer them, and some because they did not expect to suffer them: we think what is unexpected is beneath our deserts. Consequently, we are especially excited at what befalls us contrary to our hope and expectation: and this is why we are irritated at the smallest trifles in our own domestic affairs, and why we call our friends' carelessness deliberate injury. How is it, then, asks our opponent, that we are angered by the injuries inflicted by our enemies? It is because we did not expect those particular injuries, or, at any rate, not on so extensive a scale. This is caused by our excessive self-love: we think that we ought to remain uninjured even by our enemies: every man bears within his breast the mind of a despot, and is willing to commit excesses, but unwilling to submit to them. Thus it is either ignorance or arrogance that makes us angry: ignorance of common facts; for what is there to wonder at in bad men committing evil deeds? what novelty is there in your enemy hurting you, your friend quarrelling with you, your son going wrong, or your servant doing amiss? Fabius was wont to say that the most shameful excuse a general could make was "I did not think." I think it the most shameful excuse that a man can make. Think of everything, expect everything: even with men of good character something queer will crop up: human nature produces minds that are treacherous, ungrateful, greedy, and impious: when you are considering what any man's morals may be, think what those of mankind are. When you are especially enjoying yourself, be especially on your guard: when everything seems to you to be peaceful, be sure that mischief is not absent, but only asleep. Always believe that something will occur to offend you. A pilot never spreads all his canvas abroad so confidently as not to keep his tackle for shortening sail ready for use. Think, above all, bow base and hateful is the power of doing mischief, and how unnatural in man, by whose kindness even fierce animals are rendered tame. See how bulls yield their necks to the yoke, how elephants allow boys and women to dance on their backs unhurt, how snakes glide harmlessly over our bosoms and among our drinking-cups, how within their dens bears and lions submit to be handled with complacent mouths, and wild beasts fawn upon their master: let us blush to have exchanged habits with wild beasts. It is a crime to injure one's country: so it is, therefore, to injure any of our countrymen, for he is a part of our oountry; if the whole be sacred, the parts must be sacred too. Therefore it is also a crime to injure any man: for he is your fellow-citizen in a larger state. What, if the hands were to wish to hurt the feet? or the eyes to hurt the hands? As all the limbs act in unison, because it is the interest of the whole body to keep each one of them safe, so men should spare one another, because they are born for society. The bond of society, however, cannot exist unless it guards and loves all its members. We should not even destroy vipers and water-snakes and other creatures whose teeth and claws are dangerous, if we were able to tame them as we do other animals, or to prevent their befog a peril to us: neither ought we, therefore, to hurt a man because he has done wrong, but lest he should do wrong, and our punishment should always look to the future, and never to the past, because it is inflicted in a spirit of precaution, not of anger: for if everyone who has a crooked and vicious disposition were to be punished, no one would escape punishment.

XXXII.
"But anger possesses a certain pleasure of its own, and it is sweet to pay back the pain

you have suffered." Not at all; it is not honourable to requite injuries by injuries, in the same way as it is to repay benefits by benefits. In the latter case it is a shame to be conquered; in the former it is a shame to conquer. Revenge and retaliation are words which men use and even think to be righteous, yet they do not greatly differ from wrong-doing, except in the order in which they are done: he who renders pain for pain has more excuse for his sin; that is all. Someone who did not know Marcus Cato struck him in the public bath in his ignorance, for who would knowingly have done him an injury? Afterwards when he was apologizing, Cato replied, "I do not remember being struck." He thought it better to ignore the insult than to revenge it. You ask, "Did no harm befall that man for his insolence?" No, but rather much good; he made the acquaintance of Cato. It is the part of a great mind to despise wrongs done to it; the most contemptuous form of revenge is not to deem one's adversary worth taking vengeance upon. Many have taken small injuries much more seriously to heart than they need, by revenging them: that man is great and noble who like a large wild animal hears unmoved the tiny curs that bark at him.

XXXIII.

"We are treated," says our opponent," with more respect if we revenge our injuries."If we make use of revenge merely as a remedy, let us use it without anger, and not regard revenge as pleasant, but as useful: yet often it is better to pretend not to have received an injury than to avenge it. The wrongs of the powerful must not only be borne, but borne with a cheerful countenance: they will repeat the wrong if they think they have inflicted it. This is the worst trait of minds rendered arrogant by prosperity, they hate those whom they have injured. Everyone knows the saying of the old courtier, who, when someone asked him how he had achieved the rare distinction of living at court till he reached old age, replied, "By receiving wrongs and returning thanks for them." It is often so far from expedient to avenge our wrongs, that it will not do even to admit them. Gaius Caesar, offended at the smart clothes and well-dressed hair of the son of Pastor, a distinguished Roman knight, sent him to prison. When the father begged that his son might suffer no harm, Gaius, as if reminded by this to put him to death, ordered him to be executed, yet, in order to mitigate his brutality to the father, invited him that very day to dinner. Pastor came with a countenance which betrayed no ill will. Caesar pledged him in a glass of wine, and set a man to watch him. The wretched creature went through his part, feeling as though he were drinking his son's blood: the emperor sent him some perfume and a garland, and gave orders to watch whether he used them: he did so. On the very day on which he had buried, nay, on which he had not even buried his son, he sat down as one of a hundred guests, and, old and gouty as he was, drank to an extent which would have been hardly decent on a child's birthday; he shed no tear the while; he did not permit his grief to betray itself by the slightest sign; he dined just as though his entreaties had gained his son's life. You ask me why he did so? he had another son. What did Priam do in the Iliad? Did he not conceal his wrath and embrace the knees of Achilles? did he not raise to his lips that death-dealing hand, stained with the blood of his son, and sup with his slayer? True! but there were no perfumes and garlands, and his fierce enemy encouraged him with many soothing words to eat, not to drain huge goblets with a guard standing over him to see that he did it. Had he only feared for himself, the father would have treated the tyrant with scorn: but love for his son quenched his anger: he deserved the emperor's permission to leave the banquet and gather up the bones of his son: but, meanwhile, that kindly and polite youth the emperor would not even permit him to do this, but tormented the old man with frequent invitations to drink, advising him thereby to lighten his sorrows. He, on the other hand, appeared to be in good spirits, and to have forgotten what had been done that day: he would have lost his second son had he proved an unacceptable guest to the murderer of his eldest.

XXXIV.

We must, therefore, refrain from anger, whether he who provokes us be on a level with ourselves, or above us, or below us. A contest with one's equal is of uncertain issue, with one's superior is folly, and with one's inferior is contemptible. It is the part of a mean and wretched man to turn and bite one's biter: even mice and ants show their teeth if you put your hand to them, and all feeble creatures think that they are hurt if they are touched. It will make us milder tempered to call to mind any services which he with whom we are angry may have done us, and to let his deserts balance his offence. Let us also reflect, how much credit the tale of our forgiveness will confer upon us, how many men may be made into valuable friends by forgiveness. One of the lessons which Sulla's cruelty teaches us is not to be angry with the children of our enemies, whether they be public or private; for he drove the sons of the proscribed into exile. Nothing is more unjust than that any one should inherit the quarrels of his father.

Whenever we are loath to pardon anyone, let us think whether it would be to our advantage that all men should be inexorable. He who refuses to pardon, how often has he begged it for himself? how often has he grovelled at the feet of those whom he spurns from his own? How can we gain more glory than by turning anger into friendship? what more faithful allies has the Roman people than those who have been its most unyielding enemies? where would the empire be to-day, had not a wise foresight united the conquered and the conquerors? If anyone is angry with you, meet his anger by returning benefits for it: a quarrel which is only taken up on one side falls to the ground: it takes two men to fight. But suppose that there is an angry struggle on both sides, even then, he is the better man who first gives way; the winner is the real loser. He struck you; well then, do you fall back: if you strike him in turn you will give him both an opportunity and an excuse for striking you again: you will not be able to withdraw yourself from the struggle when you please.

XXXV.
Does anyone wish to strike his enemy so hard, as to leave his own hand in the wound, and not to be able, to recover his balance after the blow? yet such a weapon is anger: it is scarcely possible to draw it

back. We are careful to choose for ourselves light weapons, handy and manageable swords: shall we not avoid these clumsy, unwieldy, and never-to-be-recalled impulses of the mind? The only swiftness of which men approve is that which, when bidden, checks itself and proceeds no further, and which can be guided, and reduced from a run to a walk: we know that the sinews are diseased when they move against our will. A man must be either aged or weakly who runs when he wants to walk: let us think that those are the most powerful and the soundest operations of our minds, which act under our own control, not at their own caprice. Nothing, however, will be of so much service as to consider, first, the hideousness, and, secondly, the danger of anger. No passion bears a more troubled aspect: it befouls the fairest face, makes fierce the expression which before was peaceful. From the angry "all grace has fled;" though their clothing may be fashionable, they will trail it on the ground and take no heed of their appearance; though their hair be smoothed down in a comely manner by nature or art, yet it will bristle up in sympathy with their mind. The veins become swollen, the breast will be shaken by quick breathing, the man's neck will be swelled as he roars forth his frantic talk: then, too, his limbs will tremble, his hands will be restless, his whole body will sway hither and thither. What, think you, must be the state of his mind within him, when its appearance without is so shocking? how far more dreadful a countenance he bears within his own breast, how far keener pride, how much more violent rage, which will burst him unless it finds some vent? Let us paint anger looking like those who are dripping with the blood of foemen or savage beasts, or those who are just about to slaughter them—like those monsters of the nether world fabled by the poet to be girt with serpents and breathing flame, when they sally forth from hell, most frightful to behold, in order that they may kindle wars, stir up strife between nations, and overthrow peace; let us paint her eyes glowing with fire, her voice hissing, roaring, grating, and making worse sounds if worse there be, while she brandishes weapons in both hands, for she cares not to protect herself, gloomy, stained with blood, covered with scars and livid with her own blows, reeling like a maniac, wrapped in a thick cloud, dashing hither and thither, spreading desolation and panic, loathed by everyone and by herself above all, willing, if otherwise she cannot hurt her foe, to overthrow alike-earth, sea, and heaven, harmful and hateful at the same time. Or, if we are to see her, let her be such as our poets have described her— "There with her blood-stained scourge Bellona fights, And Discord in her riven robe delights," or, if possible, let some even more dreadful aspect be invented for this dreadful passion.

XXXVI.
Some angry people, as Sextius remarks, have been benefited by looking at the glass: they have been struck by so great an alteration in their own appearance: they have been, as it were, brought into their own presence and have not recognized themselves: yet how small a part of the real hideousness of anger did that reflected image in the mirror reproduce? Could the mind be displayed or made to appear through any substance, we should be confounded when we beheld how black and stained, how agitated, distorted, and swollen it looked: even at present if is very ugly when seen through all the screens of blood, bones, and so forth: what would it be, were it displayed uncovered? You say, that you do not believe that any one was ever scared out of anger by a mirror: and why not? because when he came to the mirror to change his mind, he had changed it already: to angry men no face looks fairer than one that is fierce and savage and such as they wish to look like. We ought rather to consider, how many men anger itself has injured. Some in their excessive heat have

burst their veins; some by straining their voices beyond their strength have vomited blood, or have injured their sight by too violently injecting humours into their eyes, and have fallen sick when the fit passed off. No way loads more swiftly to madness: many have, consequently, remained always in the frenzy of anger, and, having once lost their reason, have never recovered it. Ajax was driven mad by anger, and driven to suicide by madness. Men, frantic with rage, call upon heaven to slay their children, to reduce themselves to poverty, and to ruin their houses, and yet declare that they are not either angry or insane. Enemies to their best friends, dangerous to their nearest find dearest, regardless of the laws save where they injure, swayed by the smallest trifles, unwilling to lend their ears to the advice or the services of their friends, they do everything by main force, and are ready either to fight with their swords or to throw themselves upon them, for the greatest of all evils, and one which surpasses all vices, has gained possession of them. Other passions gain a footing in the mind by slow degrees: anger's conquest is sudden and complete, and, moreover, it makes all other passions subservient to itself. It conquers the warmest love: men have thrust swords through the bodies of those whom they loved, and have slain those in whose arms they have lain. Avarice, that sternest and most rigid of passions, is trampled underfoot by anger, which forces it to squander its carefully collected wealth and set fire to its house and all its property in one heap. Why, has not even the ambitious man been known to fling away the most highly valued ensigns of rank, and to refuse high office when it was offered to him? There is no passion over which anger does not bear absolute rule.

Footnotes
"Vehiculorum ridicule Koch," says Gertz, justly, "viliorum makes excellent sense."—J. E. B. M.

The murder of Pompeius, B.C. 48. Achillas and Theodotus acted under the nominal orders of Ptolemy XII., Cleopatra's brother, then about seventeen years of age.

The voting-place in the Campus Martius.

Ovid, Metamorphoses, i., 144, sqq. The same lines are quoted in the essay on Benefits, v. 15.

i.e., he can plead that he kept the beaten track.

De Clem. i. 12, 5

1 Compare Shakespeare, "Julius Caesar," Act v. Sc. 5: -

"His life was gentle, and the elements
So mixed in him, that nature might stand up
And say to all the world, this was a man!"
See Mr. Aldis Wright's note upon the passage.

Paedagogiis was a slave who accompanied a boy to school, &c, to keep him out of mischief; he did not teach him anything.

Tempestiva, beginning before the usual hour.

Fear of self-condemnation

Lipsius conjectures supprocax, mischievous

I have adopted the transposition of Haase and Koch

The lines are from Virgil, Æn. viii. 702, but are inaccurately quoted

BOOK 3

I.

WE will now, my Novatus, attempt to do that which you so especially long to do, that is, to drive out anger from our minds, or at all events to curb it and restrain its impulses. This may sometimes be done openly and without concealment, when we are only suffering from a slight attack of this mischief, and at other times it must be done secretly, when our anger is excessively hot, and when every obstacle thrown in its way increases it and makes it blaze higher. It is important to know how great and how fresh its strength may be, and whether it can be driven forcibly back and suppressed, or whether we must give way to it until its first storm blow over, lest it sweep away with it our remedies themselves. We must deal with each case according to each man's character: some yield to entreaties, others are rendered arrogant and masterful by submission: we may frighten some men out of their anger, while some may be turned from their purpose by reproaches, some by acknowledging oneself to be in the wrong, some by shame, and some by delay, a tardy remedy for a hasty disorder; which we ought only to use when all others have failed: for other passions admit of having their case put off, and may be healed at a later time; but the eager and self-destructive violence of anger does not grow up by slow degrees, but reaches its full height as soon as it begins. Nor does it, like other vices, merely disturb men's minds, but it takes them away, and torments them till they are incapable of restraining themselves and eager for the common ruin of all men, nor does it rage merely against its object, but against every obstacle which it encounters on its way. The other vices move our minds; anger hurls them headlong. If we are not able to withstand our passions, yet at any rate our passions ought to stand firm: but anger grows more and more powerful, like lightning flashes or hurricanes, or any other things which cannot stop themselves because they do not proceed along, but fall from above. Other vices affect our judgment, anger affects our sanity: others come in mild attacks and grow unnoticed, but men's minds plunge abruptly into anger. There is no passion that is more frantic, more destructive to its own self; it is arrogant if successful, and frantic if it fails. Even when defeated it does not grow weary, but if chance places its foe beyond its reach, it turns its teeth against itself. Its intensity is in no way regulated by its origin: for it rises to the greatest heights from the most trivial beginnings.

II.

It passes over no time of life; no race of men is exempt from it: some nations have been saved from the knowledge of luxury by the blessing of poverty; some through their active and wandering habits have escaped from sloth; those whose manners are unpolished and whose life is rustic know not chicanery and fraud and all the evils to which the courts of law give birth: but there is no race which is not excited by anger, which is equally powerful with Greeks and barbarians, and is just as ruinous among law-abiding folk as among those whose only law is that of the stronger. Finally, the other passions seize upon individuals anger is the only one which sometimes possesses a whole state. No entire people ever fell madly in love with a woman, nor did any nation ever set its affections altogether upon gain and profit. Ambition attacks single individuals; ungovernable rage is the only passion that affects nations. People often fly into a passion by troops; men and women, old men and boys, princes and populace all act alike, and the whole multitude, after being excited by a very few words, outdoes even its exciter: men betake themselves straight-way to fire and sword, and proclaim a war against their neighbours or wage one against their countrymen. Whole houses are burned with the entire families which they contain, and he who but lately was honoured for his popular eloquence now finds that his speech moves people to rage. Legions aim their darts at their commander; the whole populace quarrels with the nobles; the senate, without waiting for troops to be levied or appointing a general, hastily chooses leaders, for its anger chases well-born men through the houses of Rome, and puts them to death with its own hand. Ambassadors are outraged, the law of nations violated, and an unnatural madness seizes the state. Without allowing time for the general excitement to subside, fleets are straightway launched and laden with a hastily enrolled soldiery. Without organization, without taking any auspices, the populace rushes into the field guided only by its own anger, snatches up whatever comes first to hand by way of arms, and then atones by a great defeat for the reckless audacity of its anger. This is usually the fate of savage nations when they plunge into war: as soon as their easily excited minds are roused by the appearance of wrong having been done them, they straightway hasten forth, and, guided only by their wounded feelings, fall like an avalanche upon our legions, without either discipline, fear, or precaution, and willfully seeking for danger. They delight in being struck, in pressing forward to meet the blow, writhing their bodies along the weapon, and perishing by a wound which they themselves make.

III.

"No doubt," you say, "anger is very powerful and ruinous: point out, therefore, how it may be cured." Yet, as I stated in my former books, Aristotle stands forth in defence of anger, and forbids it to be uprooted, saying that it is the spur of virtue, and that when it is taken away, our minds become weaponless, and slow to attempt great exploits. It is therefore essential to prove its unseemliness and ferocity, and to place distinctly before our eyes how monstrous a thing it is that one man should rage against another, with what frantic violence he rushes to destroy alike himself and his foe, and overthrows those very things whose fall he himself must share. What, then? can anyone call this man sane, who, as though caught up by a hurricane, does not go but is driven, and is the slave of a senseless disorder? He does not commit to another the duty of revenging him, but himself exacts it, raging alike in thought and deed, butchering those who are dearest to him, and for whose loss he himself will ere long weep. Will any one give this passion as an assistant and companion to virtue, although it disturbs calm reason, without which virtue can do nothing? The strength which a sick man owes to a paroxysm of disease is neither lasting nor wholesome, and is strong only to its own destruction. You need not, therefore, imagine that I am wasting time over a useless task in defaming anger, as though men had not made up their minds about it, when there is someone, and he, too, an illustrious philosopher, who assigns it services to perform, and speaks of it as useful and supplying energy for battles, for the management of business, and indeed for everything which requires to be conducted with spirit. Lest it should delude any one into thinking that on certain occasions and in certain positions it may be useful, we must show its unbridled and frenzied madness, we must restore to it its attributes, the rack, the cord, the dungeon, and the cross, the fires lighted round men's buried bodies, the hook that drags both living men and corpses, the different kinds of fetters, and of punishments, the mutilations of limbs, the branding of the forehead, the dens of savage beasts. Anger should be represented as standing among these her instruments, growling in an ominous and terrible fashion, herself more shocking than any of the means by which she gives vent to her fury.

IV.
There may be some doubt about the others, but at any rate no passion has a worse look. We have described the angry man's appearance in our former books, how sharp and keen he looks, at one time

pale as his blood is driven inwards and backwards, at another with all the heat and fire of his body directed to his face, making it reddish-coloured as if stained with blood, his eyes now restless and starting out of his head, now set motionless in one fixed gaze. Add to this his teeth, which gnash against one another, as though he wished to eat somebody, with exactly the sound of a wild boar sharpening his tusks: add also the cracking of his joints, the involuntary wringing of his hands, the frequent slaps he deals himself on the chest, his hurried breathing and deep-drawn sighs, his reeling body, his abrupt broken speech, and his trembling lips, which sometimes he draws tight as he hisses some curse through them. By Hercules, no wild beast, neither when tortured by hunger, or with a weapon struck through its vitals, not even when it gathers its last breath to bite its slayer, looks so shocking as a man raging with anger. Listen, if you have leisure, to his words and threats: how dreadful is the language of his agonized mind! Would not every man wish to lay aside anger when he sees that it begins by injuring himself? When men employ anger as the most powerful of agents, consider it to be a proof of power, and reckon a speedy revenge among the greatest blessings of great prosperity, would you not wish me to warn them that he who is the slave of his own anger is not powerful, nor even free? Would you not wish me to warn all the more industrious and circumspect of men, that while other evil passions assail the base, anger gradually obtains dominion over the minds even of learned and in other respects sensible men? So true is that, that some declare anger to be a proof of straightforwardness, and it is commonly believed that the best-natured people are prone to it.

V.

You ask me, whither does all this tend? To prove, I answer, that no one should imagine himself to be safe from anger, seeing that it rouses up even those who are naturally gentle and quiet to commit savage and violent acts. As strength of body and assiduous care of the health avail nothing against a pestilence, which attacks the strong and weak alike, so also steady and good-humoured people are just as liable to attacks of anger as those of unsettled character, and in the case of the former it is both more to be ashamed of and more to be feared, because it makes a greater alteration in their habits. Now as the first thing is not to be angry, the second to lay aside our anger, and the third to be able to heal the anger of others as well as our own, I will set forth first how we may avoid falling into anger; next, how we may set ourselves free from it, and, lastly, how we may restrain an angry man, appease his wrath, and bring him back to his right mind.

We shall succeed in avoiding anger, if from time to time we lay before our minds all the vices connected with anger, and estimate it at its real value: it must be prosecuted before us and convicted: its evils must be thoroughly investigated and exposed. That we may see what it is, let it be compared with the worst vices. Avarice scrapes together and amasses riches for some better man to use: anger spends money; few can indulge in it for nothing. How many slaves an angry master drives to run away or to commit suicide! how much more he loses by his anger than the value of what he originally became angry about! Anger brings grief to a father, divorce to a husband, hatred to a magistrate, failure to a candidate for office. It is worse than luxury, because luxury enjoys its own pleasure, while anger enjoys another's pain. It is worse than either spitefulness or envy; for they wish that someone may become unhappy, while anger wishes to make him so: they are pleased when evil befalls one by accident, but anger cannot wait upon Fortune; it desires to injure its victim personally, and is not satisfied merely with his being injured. Nothing is more dangerous than jealousy: it is produced by anger. Nothing is more ruinous than war: it is the outcome of powerful men's anger; and even the anger of humble private persons, though without arms or armies, is nevertheless war. Moreover, even if we pass over its immediate consequences, such as heavy losses, treacherous plots, and the constant anxiety produced by strife, anger pays a penalty at the same moment that it exacts one: it forswears human feelings. The latter urge us to love, anger urges us to hatred: the latter bid us do men good, anger bids us do them harm. Add to this that, although its rage arises from an excessive self-respect and appears to show high spirit, it really is contemptible and mean: for a man must be inferior to one by whom he thinks himself despised, whereas the truly great mind, which takes a true estimate of its own value, does not revenge an insult because it does not feel it. As weapons rebound from a hard surface, and solid substances hurt those who strike them, so also no insult can make a really great mind sensible of its presence, being weaker than that against which it is aimed. How far more glorious is it to throw back all wrongs and insults from oneself, like one wearing armour of proof against all weapons, for revenge is an admission that we have been hurt. That cannot be a great mind which is disturbed by injury. He who has hurt you must be either stronger or weaker than yourself. If he be weaker, spare him: if he be stronger, spare yourself.

VI.

There is no greater proof of magnanimity than that nothing which befalls you should be able to move you to anger. The higher region of the universe, being more excellently ordered and near to the stars, is never gathered into clouds, driven about by storms, or whirled round by cyclones: it is free from all disturbance: the lightnings flash in the region below it. In like manner a lofty mind, always placid and dwelling in a serene atmosphere, restraining within itself all the impulses from which anger springs, is modest, commands respect, and remains calm and collected: none of which qualities will you find in an angry man: for who, when under the influence of grief and rage, does not first get rid of bashfulness? who, when excited and confused and about to attack someone, does not fling away any habits of shamefacedness he may have possessed? what angry man attends to the number or routine of his duties? who uses moderate language? Who keeps any part of his body quiet? who can guide himself when in full career? We shall find much profit in that sound maxim of Democritus which defines peace of mind to consist in not labouring much, or too much for our strength, either in public or private matters. A man's day, if he is engaged in many various occupations, never passes so happily that no man or no thing should give rise to some offence which makes the mind ripe for anger. Just as when one hurries through the crowded parts of the city one cannot help jostling many people, and one cannot help slipping at one place, being hindered at another, and splashed at another, so when one's life is spent in disconnected pursuits and wanderings, one must meet with many troubles and many accusations. One man deceives our hopes, another delays their fulfillment, another destroys them: our projects do not proceed according to our intention. No one is so favoured by Fortune as to find her always on his side if he tempts her often: and from this it follows that he who sees several enterprises turn out contrary to his wishes becomes dissatisfied with both men and things, and on the slightest provocation flies into a rage with people, with undertakings, with places, with fortune, or with himself. In order, therefore, that the mind may be at peace, it ought not to be hurried hither and thither, nor, as I said before, wearied by labour at great matters, or matters whose attainment is beyond its strength. It is easy to fit one's shoulder to a light burden, and to shift it from one side to the other without dropping it: but we have difficulty in bearing the burdens which others' hands lay upon us, and when overweighted by them we fling them off upon our neighbours. Even when we do stand upright under our load, we nevertheless reel beneath a weight which is beyond our strength.

VII.
Be assured that the same rule applies both to public and private life: simple and manageable undertakings proceed according to the pleasure of the person in charge of them, but enormous ones, beyond his capacity to manage, are not easily undertaken. When he has got them to administer, they hinder him, and press hard upon him, and just as he thinks that success is within his grasp, they collapse, and carry him with them: ==thus it comes about that a man's wishes are often disappointed if he does not apply himself to easy tasks, yet wishes that the tasks which he undertakes may be easy==. Whenever you would attempt anything, first form an estimate both of your own powers, of the extent of the matter which you are undertaking, and of the means by which you are to accomplish it: for if you have to abandon your work when it is half done, ==the disappointment will sour your temper.== In such cases, it makes a difference whether one is of an ardent or of a cold and unenterprising temperament: ==for failure will rouse a generous spirit to anger, and will move a sluggish and dull one to sorrow. Let our undertakings, therefore, be neither petty nor yet presumptuous and==

reckless: let our hopes not range far from home: let us attempt nothing which if we succeed will make us astonished at our success.

VIII.
Since we know not how to endure an injury, let us take care not to receive one: we should live with the quietest and easiest-tempered persons, not with anxious or with sullen ones: for our own habits are copied from those with whom we associate, and just as some bodily diseases are communicated by touch, so also the mind transfers its vices to its neighbours. A drunkard leads even those who reproach him to grow fond of wine: profligate society will, if permitted, impair the morals even of robust-minded men: avarice infects those nearest it with its poison. Virtues do the same thing in the opposite direction, and improve all those with whom they are brought in contact: it is as good for one of unsettled principles to associate with better men than himself as for an invalid to live in a warm country with a healthy climate. You will understand how much may be effected this way, if you observe how even wild beasts grow tame by dwelling among us, and how no animal, however ferocious, continues to be wild, if it has long been accustomed to human companionship: all its savageness becomes softened, and

amid peaceful scenes is gradually forgotten. We must add to this, that the man who lives with quiet people is not only improved by their example, but also by the fact that he finds no reason for anger and does not practise his vice: it will, therefore, be his duty to avoid all those who he knows will excite his anger. You ask, who these are: many will bring about the same thing by various means; a proud man will offend you by his disdain, a talkative man by his abuse, an impudent man by his insults, a spiteful man by his malice, a quarrelsome man by his wrangling, a braggart and liar by his vaingloriousness: you will not endure to be feared by a suspicious man, conquered by an obstinate one, or scorned by an ultra-refined one: Choose straightforward, good-natured, steady people, who will not provoke your wrath, and will bear with it. Those whose dispositions are yielding, polite and suave, will be of even greater service, provided they do not flatter, for excessive obsequiousness irritates bad-tempered men. One of my own friends was a good man indeed, but too prone to anger, and it was as dangerous to flatter him as to curse him. Caelius the orator, it is well known, was the worst-tempered man possible. It is said that once he was dining in his own chamber with an especially long-suffering client, but had great difficulty when thrown thus into a man's society to avoid quarrelling with him.

The other thought it best to agree to whatever he said, and to play second fiddle, but Caelius could not bear his obsequious agreement, and exclaimed, "Do contradict me in something, that there may be two of us!" Yet even he, who was angry at not being angry, soon recovered his temper, because he had no one to fight with. If, then, we are conscious of an irascible disposition, let us especially choose for our friends those who will look and speak as we do: they will pamper us and lead us into a bad habit of listening to nothing that does not please us, but it will be good to give our anger respite and repose. Even those who are naturally crabbed and wild will yield to caresses: no creature continues either angry or frightened if you pat him. Whenever a controversy seems likely to be longer or more keenly disputed than usual, let us check its first beginnings, before it gathers strength. A dispute nourishes itself as it proceeds, and takes hold of those who plunge too deeply into it: it is easier to stand aloof than to extricate oneself from a struggle.

IX.
Irascible men ought not to meddle with the more serious class of occupations, or, at any rate, ought to stop short of weariness in the pursuit of them; their mind ought not to be engaged upon hard subjects, but

handed over to pleasing arts: let it be softened by reading poetry, and interested by legendary history: let it be treated with luxury and refinement. Pythagoras used to calm his troubled spirit by playing upon the lyre: and who does not know that trumpets and clarions are irritants, just as some airs are lullabies and soothe the mind? Green is good for wearied eyes, and some colours are grateful to weak sight, while the brightness of others is painful to it. In the same way cheerful pursuits soothe unhealthy minds. We must avoid law courts, pleadings, verdicts, and everything else that aggravates our fault, and we ought no less to avoid bodily weariness; for it exhausts all that is quiet and gentle in us, and rouses bitterness. For this reason those who cannot trust their digestion, when they are about to transact business of importance always allay their bile with food, for it is peculiarly irritated by fatigue, either because it draws the vital heat into the middle of the body, and injures the blood and stops its circulation by the clogging of the veins, or else because the worn-out and weakened body reacts upon the mind: this is certainly the reason why those who are broken by ill health or age are more irascible than other men. Hunger also and thirst should be avoided for the same reason; they exasperate and irritate men's minds: it is an old saying that "a weary man is quarrelsome

": and so also is a hungry or a thirsty man, or one who is suffering from any cause whatever: for just as sores pain one at the slightest touch, and afterwards even at the fear of being touched, so an unsound mind takes offence at the slightest things, so that even a greeting, a letter, a speech, or a question, provokes some men to anger.

X.
That which is diseased can never bear to be handled without complaining: it is best, therefore, to apply remedies to oneself as soon as we feel that anything is wrong, to allow oneself as little licence as possible in speech, and to restrain one's impetuosity: now it is easy to detect the first growth of our passions: the symptoms precede the disorder. Just as the signs of storms and rain come before the storms themselves, so there are certain forerunners of anger, love, and all the storms which torment our minds. Those who suffer from epilepsy know that the fit is coming on if their extremities become cold, their sight fails, their sinews tremble, their memory deserts them, and their head swims: they accordingly check the growing disorder by applying the usual remedies: they try to prevent the loss of their senses by smelling or tasting some drug; they battle against cold and stiffness of limbs by hot fomentations; or, if all remedies fail, they retire apart, and faint

where no one sees them fall. It is useful for a man to understand his disease, and to break its strength before it becomes developed. Let us see what it is that especially irritates us. Some men take offence at insulting words, others at deeds: one wishes his pedigree, another his person, to be treated with respect. This man wishes to be considered especially fashionable, that man to be thought especially learned: one cannot bear pride, another cannot bear obstinacy. One thinks it beneath him to be angry with his slaves, another is cruel at home, but gentle abroad. One imagines that he is proposed for office because he is unpopular, another thinks himself insulted because he is not proposed. People do not all take offence in the same way; you ought then to know what your own weak point is, that you may guard it with especial care.

XI.
It is better not to see or to hear everything: many causes of offence may pass by us, most of which are disregarded by the man who ignores them. Would you not be irascible? then be not inquisitive. He who seeks to know what is said about him, who digs up spiteful tales even if they were told in secret, is himself the destroyer of his own peace of mind. Some stories may be so construed as to appear to be insults:

wherefore it is best to put some aside, to laugh at others, and to pardon others. There are many ways in which anger may be checked; most things may be turned into jest. It is said that Socrates when he was given a box on the ear, merely said that it was a pity a man could not tell when he ought to wear his helmet out walking. It does not so much matter how an injury is done, as how it is borne; and I do not see how moderation can be hard to practise, when I know that even despots, though success and impunity combine to swell their pride, have sometimes restrained their natural ferocity. At any rate, tradition informs us that once, when a guest in his cups bitterly reproached Pisistratus, the despot of Athens, for his cruelty, many of those present offered to lay hands on the traitor, and one said one thing and one another to kindle his wrath, he bore it coolly, and replied to those who were egging him on, that he was no more angry with the man than he should be with one who ran against him blindfold.

XII.
A large part of mankind manufacture their own grievances either by entertaining unfounded suspicions or by exaggerating trifles. Anger often comes to us, but we often go to it. It ought never to be sent for: even when it falls in our way it ought to be

flung aside. No one says to himself, "I myself have done or might have done this very thing which I am angry with another for doing." No one considers the intention of the doer, but merely the thing done . yet we ought to think about him, and whether he did it intentionally or accidentally, under compulsion or under a mistake, whether he did it out of hatred for us, or to gain something for himself, whether he did it to please himself or to serve a friend. In some cases the age, in others the worldly fortunes of the culprit may render it humane or advantageous to bear with him and put up with what he has done. Let us put ourselves in the place of him with whom we are angry: at present an overweening conceit of our own importance makes us prone to anger, and we are quite willing to do to others what we cannot endure should be done to ourselves. No one will postpone his anger: yet delay is the best remedy for it, because it allows its first glow to subside, and gives time for the cloud which darkens the mind either to disperse or at any rate to become less dense. Of these wrongs which drive you frantic, some will grow lighter after an interval, not of a day, but even of an hour: some will vanish altogether. Even if you gain nothing by your adjournment, still what you do after it will appear to be the result of mature deliberation, not of anger. If you want to find out the truth about anything, commit the task to time: nothing can be accurately discerned at a time of disturbance. Plato, when angry with his slave, could not prevail upon himself to wait, but straightway ordered him to take off his shirt and present his shoulders to the blows which he meant to give him with his own hand: then, when he perceived that he was angry, he stopped the hand which he had raised in the air, and stood like one in act to strike. Being asked by a friend who happened to come in, what he was doing, he answered: "I am making an angry man expiate his crime." He retained the posture of one about to give way to passion, as if struck with astonishment at its being so degrading to a philosopher, forgetting the slave, because he had found another still more deserving of punishment. He therefore denied himself the exercise of authority over his own household, and once, being rather angry at some fault, said, "Speusippus, will you please to correct that slave with stripes; for I am in a rage." He would not strike him, for the very reason for which another man would have struck him. "I am in a rage," said he; "I should beat him more than I ought: I should take more pleasure than I ought in doing so: let not that slave fall into the power of one who is not in his own power." Can anyone wish to grant the power of revenge to an angry man, when Plato himself gave up his own right to exercise it? While you are angry, you ought not to be allowed to do anything. "Why?" do you ask? Because when you are angry there is nothing that you do not wish to be allowed to do.

XIII.
Fight hard with yourself and if you cannot conquer anger, do not let it conquer you: you have begun to get the better of it if it does not show itself, if it is not given vent. Let us conceal its symptoms, and as far as possible keep it secret and hidden. It will give us great trouble to do this, for it is eager to burst forth, to kindle our eyes and to transform our face; but if we allow it to show itself in our outward appearance, it is our master. Let it rather be locked in the innermost recesses of our breast, and be borne by us, not bear us: nay, let us replace all its symptoms by their opposites; let us make our countenance more composed than usual, our voice milder, our step slower. Our inward thoughts gradually become influenced by our outward demeanour. With Socrates it was a sign of anger when he lowered his voice, and became sparing of speech; it was evident at such times that he was exercising restraint over himself. His friends, consequently, used to detect him acting thus, and convict him of being angry; nor was he displeased at being charged with concealment of

anger; indeed, how could he help being glad that many men should perceive his anger, yet that none should feel it? they would however, have felt it had not he granted to his friends the same right of criticizing his own conduct which he himself assumed over theirs. How much more needful is it for us to do this? let us beg all our best friends to give us their opinion with the greatest freedom at the very time when we can bear it least, and never to be compliant with us when we are angry. While we are in our right senses, while we are under our own control, let us call for help against so powerful an evil, and one which we regard with such unjust favour. Those who cannot carry their wine discreetly, and fear to be betrayed into some rash and insolent act, give their slaves orders to take them away from the banquet when they are drunk; those who know by experience how unreasonable they are when sick give orders that no one is to obey them when they are in ill health. It is best to prepare obstacles beforehand for vices which are known, and above all things so to tranquilize our mind that it may bear the most sudden and violent shocks either without feeling anger, or, if anger be provoked by the extent of some unexpected wrong, that it may bury it deep, and not betray its wound. That it is possible to do this will be seen, if I quote a few of an abundance of examples, from which we may learn both how much evil there is in anger, when it exercises entire dominion over men in supreme power, and how completely it can control itself when overawed by fear.

XIV.
King Cambyses was excessively addicted to wine. Præxaspes was the only one of his closest friends who advised him to drink more sparingly, pointing out how shameful a thing drunkenness was in a king, upon whom all eyes and ears were fixed. Cambyses answered, "That you may know that I never lose command of myself, I will presently prove to you that both my eyes and my hands are fit for service after I have been drinking." Hereupon he drank more freely than usual, using larger cups, and when heavy and besotted with wine ordered his reprover's son to go beyond the threshold and stand there with his left hand raised above his head; then he bent his bow and pierced the youth's heart, at which he had said that he aimed. He then had his. breast cut open, showed the arrow sticking exactly into the heart, and, looking at the boy's father, risked whether his hand was not steady enough. He replied, that Apollo himself could not have taken better aim. God confound such a man, a slave in mind, if not in station! He actually praised an act which he ought not to have endured to

witness. He thought that the breast of his son being torn asunder, and his heart quivering with its wound, gave him an opportunity of making a complimentary speech. He ought to have raised a dispute with him about his success, and have called for another shot, that the king might be pleased to prove upon the person of the father that his hand was even steadier than when he shot the son. What a savage king! what a worthy mark for all his follower's arrows! Yet though we curse him for making his banquet end in cruelty and death, still it was worse to praise that arrow-shot than to shoot it. We shall see hereafter how a father ought to bear himself when standing over the corpse of his son, whose murder he had both caused and witnessed: the matter which we are now discussing, has been proved, I mean, that anger can be suppressed. He did not curse the king, he did not so much as let fall a single inauspicious word, though he felt his own heart as deeply wounded as that of his son. He may be said to have done well in choking down his words; for though he might have spoken as an angry man, yet he could not have expressed what he felt as a father. He may, I repeat, be thought to have behaved with greater wisdom on that occasion than when he tried to regulate the drink of one who was better employed in drinking wine than in drinking blood, and who granted men peace while his hands were busy with the winecup. He, therefore, added one more to the number of those who have shown to their bitter cost how little kings care for their friends' good advice.

XV.
I have no doubt that Harpagus must have given some such advice to the king of the Persians and of himself, in anger at which the king placed Harpagus's own children before him on the dinner-table for him to eat, and asked him from time to time, whether he liked the seasoning. Then, when he saw that he was satiated with his own misery, he ordered their heads to be brought to him, and asked him how he liked his entertainment. The wretched man did not lose his readiness of speech; his face did not change. "Every kind of dinner," said he, "is pleasant at the king's table." What did he gain by this obsequiousness? He avoided being invited a second time to dinner, to eat what was left of them. I do not forbid a father to blame the act of his king, or to seek for some revenge worthy of so bloodthirsty a monster, but in the meanwhile I gather from the tale this fact, that even the anger which arises from unheard of outrages can be concealed, and forced into using language which is the very reverse of its meaning. This way of curbing anger is necessary, at least for those who have

chosen this sort of life and who are admitted to dine at a king's table; this is how they must eat and drink, this is how they must answer, and how they must laugh at their own deaths. Whether life is worth having at such a price, we shall see hereafter; that is another question. Let us not console so sorry a crew, or encourage them to submit to the orders of their butchers; let us point out that however slavish a man's condition may be, there is always a path to liberty open to him, unless his mind be diseased. It is a man's own fault if he suffers, when by putting an end to himself he can put an end to his misery. To him whose king aimed arrows at the breasts of his friends, and to him whose master gorged fathers with the hearts of their children, I would say "Madman, why do you groan? for what are you waiting? for some enemy to avenge you by the destruction of your entire nation, or for some powerful king to arrive from a distant land? Wherever you turn your eyes you may see an end to your woes. Do you see that precipice? Down that lies the road to liberty; do you see that sea? that river? that well? Liberty sits at the bottom of them. Do you see that tree? stunted, blighted, dried up though it be, yet liberty hangs from its branches. Do you see your own throat, your own neck, your own heart? they are so many ways of escape from slavery. Are these modes which I point out too laborious, and needing much strength and courage? do you ask what path leads to liberty? I answer, any vein in your body.

XVI.
As long, however, as we find nothing in our life so unbearable as to drive us to suicide, let us, in whatever position we may be, set anger far from us: it is destructive to those who are its slaves. All its rage turns to its own misery, and authority becomes all the more irksome the more obstinately it is resisted. It is like a wild animal whose struggles only pull the noose by which it is caught tighter; or like birds who, while flurriedly trying to shake themselves free, smear birdlime onto all their feathers. No yoke is so grievous as not to hurt him who struggles against it more than him who yields to it: the only way to alleviate great evils is to endure them and to submit to do what they compel. This control of our passions, and especially of this mad and unbridled passion of anger, is useful to subjects, but still more useful to kings. All is lost when a man's position enables him to carry out whatever anger prompts him to do; nor can power long endure if it be exercised to the injury of many, for it becomes endangered as soon as common fear draws together those who bewail themselves separately. Many kings,

therefore, have fallen victims, some to single individuals, others to entire peoples, who have been forced by general indignation to make one man the minister of their wrath. Yet many kings have indulged their anger as though it were a privilege of royalty, like Darius, who, after the dethronement of the Magian, was the first ruler of the Persians and of the greater part of the East: for when he declared war against the Scythians who bordered on the empire of the East, Oeobazus, an aged noble, begged that one of his three sons might be left at home to comfort his father, and that the king might be satisfied with the services of two of them. Darius promised him more than he asked for, saying that he would allow all three to remain at home, and flung their dead bodies before their father's eyes. He would have been harsh, had he taken them all to the war with him. How much more good-natured was Xerxes, who, when Pythias, the father of five sons, begged for one to be excused from service, permitted him to choose which he wished for. He then tore the son whom the father had chosen into two halves, placed one on each side of the road, and, as it were, purified his army by means of this propitiatory victim. He therefore had the end which he deserved, being defeated, and his army scattered far and wide in utter rout, while he in the midst of it walked among the corpses of his soldiers, seeing on all sides the signs of his own overthrow.

XVII.
So ferocious in their anger were those kings who had no learning, no tincture of polite literature: now I will show you King Alexander (the Great), fresh from the lap of Aristotle, who with his own hand while at table stabbed Clitus, his dearest friend, who had been brought up with him, because he did not flatter him enough, and was too slow in transforming himself from a free man and a Macedonian into a Persian slave. Indeed he shut up Lysimachus, who was no less his friend than Clitus, in a cage with a lion; yet did this make Lysimachus, who escaped by some happy chance from the lion's teeth, any gentler when he became a king? Why, he mutilated his own friend, Telesphorus the Rhodian, cutting off his nose and ears, and kept him for a long while in a den, like some new and strange animal, after the hideousness of his hacked and disfigured face had made him no longer appear to be human, assisted by starvation and the squalid filth of a body loft to wallow in its own dung! Besides this, his hands and knees, which the narrowness of his abode forced him to use instead of his feet, became hard and callous, while his sides were covered with sores by rubbing against the walls, so that his appearance was no less shocking

than frightful, and his punishment turned him into so monstrous a creature that he was not even pitied. Yet, however unlike a man he was who suffered this, even more unlike was he who inflicted it.

XVIII.
Would to heaven that such savagery had contented itself with foreign examples, and that barbarity in anger and punishment had not been imported with other outlandish vices into our Roman manners! Marcus Marius, to whom the people erected a statue in every street, to whom they made offerings of incense and wine, had, by the command of Lucius Sulla, his legs broken, his eyes pulled out, his hands cut off, and his whole body gradually torn to pieces limb by limb, as if Sulla killed him as many times as he wounded him. Who was it who carried out Sulla's orders? who but Catiline, already practising his hands in every sort of wickedness? He tore him to pieces before the tomb of Quintus Catulus, an unwelcome burden to the ashes of that gentlest of men, above which one who was no doubt a criminal, yet nevertheless the idol of the people, and who was not undeserving of love, although men loved him beyond all reason, was forced to shed his blood drop by drop. Though Marius deserved such tortures, yet it was worthy of Sulla to order them, and of Catiline to execute them; but it

was unworthy of the State to be stabbed by the swords of her enemy and her avenger alike. Why do I pry into ancient history? quite lately Gaius Caesar flogged and tortured Sextus Papinius, whose father was a consular, Betilienas Bassus, his own quaestor, and several others, both senators and knights, on the same day, not to carry out any judicial inquiry, but merely to amuse himself. Indeed, so impatient was he of any delay in receiving the pleasure which his monstrous cruelty never delayed in asking, that when walking with some ladies and senators in his mother's gardens, along the walk between the colonnade and the river, he struck off some of their heads by lamplight. What did he fear? what public or private danger could one night threaten him with? how very small a favour it would have been to wait until morning, and not to kill the Roman people's senators in his slippers?

XIX.
It is to the purpose that we should know how haughtily his cruelty was exercised, although someone might suppose that we are wandering from the subject and embarking on a digression; but this digression is itself connected with unusual outbursts of anger. He beat senators with rods; he did it so often that he made men able to say, "It is the custom." He tortured them with all the most dismal engines in the

world, with the cord, the boots, the rack, the fire, and the sight of his own face. Even to this we may answer, " To tear three senators to pieces with stripes and fire like criminal slaves was no such great crime for one who had thoughts of butchering the entire Senate, who was wont to wish that the Roman people had but one neck, that he might concentrate into one day and one blow all the wickedness which he divided among so many places and times. Was there ever anything so unheard-of as an execution in the night-time? Highway robbery seeks for the shelter of darkness, but the more public an execution is, the more power it has as an example and lesson. Here I shall be met by: "This, which you are so surprised at, was the daily habit of that monster; this was what he lived for, watched for, sat up at night for." Certainly one could find no one else who would have ordered all those whom he condemned to death to have their mouths closed by a sponge being fastened in them, that they might not have the power even of uttering a sound. What dying man was ever forbidden to groan? He feared that the last agony might find too free a voice, that he might hear what would displease him. He knew, moreover, that there were countless crimes, with which none but a dying man would dare to reproach him. When sponges were not forthcoming, he ordered the wretched men's clothes to be torn up, and the rags stuffed into their mouths. What savagery was this? Let a man draw his last breath: give room for his soul to escape through: let it not be forced to leave the body through a wound. It becomes tedious to add to this that in the same night he sent centurions to the houses of the executed men and made an end of their fathers also, that is to say, being a compassionate-minded man, he set them free from sorrow: for it is not my intention to describe the ferocity of Gaius, but the ferocity of anger, which does not merely vent its rage upon individuals, but rends in pieces whole nations, and even lashes cities, rivers, and things which have no sense of pain.

XX.
Thus, the king of the Persians cut off the noses of a whole nation in Syria, wherefore the place is called Rhinocolura. Do you think that he was merciful, because he did not cut their heads off altogether? no, he was delighted at having invented a new kind of punishment. Something of the same kind would have befallen the Æthiopians, who on account of their prodigiously long lives are called Macrobiotae; for, because they did not receive slavery with hands uplifted to heaven in thankfulness, and sent an embassy which used independent, or what kings call insulting language, Cambyses

became wild with rage, and, without any store of provisions, or any knowledge of the roads, started with all his fighting men through an arid and trackless waste, where during the first day's march the necessaries of life failed, and the country itself furnished nothing, being barren and uncultivated, and untrodden by the foot of man. At first the tenderest parts of leaves and shoots of trees relieved their hunger, then hides softened by fire, and anything else that their extremity drove them to use as food. When as they proceeded neither roots nor herbs were to be found in the sand, and they found a wilderness destitute even of animal life, they chose each tenth man by lot and made of him a meal which was more cruel than hunger. Rage still drove the king madly forwards, until after he had lost one part of his army and eaten another he began to fear that he also might be called upon to draw the lot for his life; then at last he gave the order for retreat. Yet all the while his well-bred hawks were not sacrificed, and the means of feasting were carried for him on camels, while his soldiers were drawing lots for who should miserably perish, and who should yet more miserably live.

XXI.
This man was angry with an unknown and inoffensive nation, which nevertheless was able to feel his wrath; but Cyrus was angry

with a river. When hurrying to besiege Babylon, since in making war it is above all things important to seize one's opportunity, he tried to ford the wide-spread river Gyndes, which it is hardly safe to attempt even when the river has been dried up by the summer heat and is at its lowest. Here one of the white horses which drew the royal chariot was washed away, and his loss moved the king to such violent rage, that he swore to reduce the river which had carried off his royal retinue to so low an ebb that even women should walk across it and trample upon it. He thereupon devoted all the resources of his army to this object, and remained working until by cutting one hundred and eighty channels across the bed of the river he divided it into three hundred and sixty brooks, and left the bed dry, the waters flowing through other channels. Thus he lost time, which is very important in great operations, and lost, also, the soldiers' courage, which was broken by useless labour, and the opportunity of falling upon his enemy unprepared, while he was waging against the river the war which he had declared against his foes. This frenzy, for what else can you call it, has befallen Romans also, for G. Caesar destroyed a most beautiful villa at Herculaneum because his mother was once imprisoned in it, and has thus made the place notorious by its misfortune; for while it stood, we used to sail past it without noticing it, but now people inquire why it is in ruins.

XXII.
These should be regarded as examples to be avoided, and what I am about to relate, on the contrary, to be followed, being examples of gentle and lenient conduct in men who both had reasons for anger and power to avenge themselves. What could have been easier than for Antigonus to order those two common soldiers to be executed who leaned against their king's tent while doing what all men especially love to do, and run the greatest danger by doing, I mean while they spoke evil of their king. Antigonus heard all they said, as was likely, since there was only a piece of cloth between the speakers and the listener, who gently raised it, .and said "Go a little further off, for fear the king should hear you." He also on one night, hearing some of his soldiers invoking everything that was evil upon their king for having brought them along that road and into that impassable mud, went to those who were in the greatest difficulties, and having extricated them without their knowing who was their helper, said, "Now curse Antigonus, by whose fault you have fallen into this trouble, but bless the man who has brought you out of this slough." This same Antigonus bore the abuse of his enemies as good-naturedly

as that of his countrymen; thus when he was besieging some Greeks in a little fort, and they, despising their enemy through their confidence in the strength of their position, cut many jokes upon the ugliness of Antigonus, at one time mocking him for his shortness of stature, at another for his broken nose, he answered, "I rejoice, and expect some good fortune because I have a Silenus in my camp." After he had conquered these witty folk by hunger, his treatment of them was to form regiments of those who were fit for service, and sell the rest by public auction; nor would he, said he, have done this had it not been better that men who had such evil tongues should be under the control of a master.

XXIII.
This man's grandson was Alexander, who used to hurl his lance at his guests, who, of the two friends which I have mentioned above, exposed one to the rage of a wild beast, and the other to his own; yet of these two men, he who was exposed to the lion survived. He did not derive this vice from his grandfather, nor even from his father; for it was an especial virtue of Philip's to endure insults patiently, and was a great safeguard of his kingdom. Demochares, who was surnamed Parrhesiastes on account of his unbridled and impudent tongue, came on an embassy to him with other ambassadors

from Athens. After graciously listening to what they had to say, Philip said to them, "Tell me, what can I do that will please the Athenians?" Demochares took him up, and answered, "Hang yourself." All the bystanders expressed their indignation at so brutal an answer, but Philip bade them be silent, and let this Thersites depart safe and sound. "But do you," said he, "you other ambassadors, tell the Athenians that those who say such things are much more arrogant than those who hear them without revenging themselves." The late Emperor Augustus also did and said many memorable things, which prove that he was not under the dominion of anger. Timagenes, the historical writer, made some remarks upon him, his wife, and his whole family: nor did his jests fall to the ground, for nothing spreads more widely or is more in people's mouths than reckless wit. Caesar often warned him to be less audacious in his talk, and as he continued to offend, forbade him his house. Timagenes after this passed the later years of his life as the guest of Asinius Pollio, and was the favourite of the whole city: the closing of Caesar's door did not close any other door against him. He read aloud the history which he wrote after this, but burned the books which contained the doings of Augustus Caesar. He was at enmity with Caesar, but yet no one feared to be his friend, no one shrank from him as though he were blasted by lightning: although he fell from so high a place, yet someone was found to catch him in his lap. Caesar, I say, bore this with patience, and was not even irritated by the historian's having laid violent hands upon his own glories and acts: he never complained of the man who afforded his enemy shelter, but merely said to Asinius Pollio "You are keeping a wild beast:" then, when the other would have excused his conduct, he stopped him, and said "Enjoy, my Pollio, enjoy his friendship." When Pollio said, "If you order me, Caesar, I will straightway forbid him my house," he answered, "Do you think that I am likely to do this, after having made you friends again?" for formerly Pollio had been angry with Timagenes, and ceased to be angry with him for no other reason than that Caesar began to be so.

XXIV.
Let everyone, then, say to himself, whenever he is provoked, "Am I more powerful than Philip? yet he allowed a man to curse him with impunity. Have I more authority in my own house than the Emperor Augustus possessed throughout the world? yet he was satisfied with leaving the society of his maligner. Why should I make my slave atone by stripes and manacles for having answered me too

loudly or having put on a stubborn look, or muttered something which I did not catch? Who am I, that it should be a crime to shock my ears? Many men have forgiven their enemies: shall I not forgive men for being lazy, careless, and gossipping?" We ought to plead age as an excuse for children, sex for women, freedom for a stranger, familiarity for a house-servant. Is this his first offence? think how long he has been acceptable. Has he often done wrong, and in many other cases? then let us continue to bear what we have borne so long. Is he a friend? then he did not intend to do it. Is he an enemy? then in doing it he did his duty. If he be a sensible man, let us believe his excuses; if a fool, let us grant him pardon; whatever he may be, let us say to ourselves on his behalf, that even the wisest of men are often in fault, that no one is so alert that his carefulness never betrays itself, that no one is of so ripe a judgment that his serious mind cannot be goaded by circumstances into some hotheaded action, that, in fine, no one, however much he may fear to give offence, can help doing so even while he tries to avoid it.

XXV.

As it is a consolation to a humble man in trouble that the greatest are subject to reverses of fortune, and a man weeps more calmly over his dead son in the corner of his hovel if he sees a piteous funeral proceed out of the palace as well; so one bears injury or insult more calmly if one remembers that no power is so great as to be above the reach of harm. Indeed, if even the wisest do wrong, who cannot plead a good excuse for his faults? Let us look back upon our own youth, and think how often we then were too slothful in our duty, too impudent in our speech, too intemperate in our cups. Is anyone angry then let us give him enough time to reflect upon what he has done, and he will correct his own self. But suppose he ought to pay the penalty of his deeds: well, that is no reason why we should act as he does. It cannot be doubted that he who regards his tormentor with contempt raises himself above the common herd and looks down upon them from a loftier position: it is the property of true magnanimity not to feel the blows which it may receive. So does a huge wild beast turn slowly and gaze at yelping curs: so does the wave dash in vain against a great cliff. The man who is not angry remains unshaken by injury: he who is angry has been moved by it. He, however, whom I have described as being placed too high for any mischief to reach him, holds as it were the highest good in his arms: he can reply, not only to any man, but to fortune herself: "Do what you will, you are too feeble to disturb my serenity: this is forbidden by reason, to whom I have entrusted the guidance of my life: to become angry would do me more harm than your violence can do me. 'More harm?' say you. Yes, certainly: I know how much injury you have done me, but I cannot tell to what excesses anger might not carry me."

XXVI.
You say, "I cannot endure it: injuries are hard to bear." You lie; for how can anyone not be able to bear injury, if he can bear to be angry? Besides, what you intend to do is to endure both injury and anger. Why do you bear with the delirium of a sick man, or the ravings of a madman, or the impudent blows of a child? Because, of course, they evidently do not know what they are doing: a man be not responsible for his actions, what does it matter by what malady he became so : the plea of ignorance holds equally good in every case. "What then?" say you, "shall he not be punished?" He will be, even supposing that you do not wish it: for the greatest punishment for having done harm is the sense of having done it, and no one is more severely punished than he who is given over to the punishment of remorse. In the next place, we ought to conder the whole state of mankind, in order to pass a just judgment on all the occurrences of life: for it is unjust to blame individuals for a vice which is common to all. The colour of an Æthiop is not remarkable among this own

people, nor is any man in Germany ashamed of red hair rolled into a knot. You cannot call anything peculiar or disgraceful in a particular man if it is the general characteristic of his nation. Now, the cases which I have quoted are defended only by the usage of one out-of-the-way quarter of the world: see now, how far more deserving of pardon those crimes are which are spread abroad among all mankind. We all are hasty and careless, we all are untrustworthy, dissatisfied, and ambitious: nay, why do I try to hide our common wickedness by a too partial description? we all are bad. Every one of us therefore will find in his own breast the vice which he blames in another. Why do you remark how pale this man, or how lean that man is? there is a general pestilence. Let us therefore be more gentle one to another: we are bad men, living among bad men: there is only one thing which can afford us peace, and that is to agree to forgive one another. "This man has already injured me," say you, "and I have not yet injured him." No, but you have probably injured someone else, and you will injure him some day. Do not form your judgment by one hour, or one day: consider the whole tendency of your mind: even though you have done no evil, yet you are capable of doing it.

XXVII.

How far better is it to heal an injury than to avenge it? Revenge takes up much time, and throws itself in the way of many injuries while it is smarting under one. We all retain our anger longer than we feel our hurt: how far better it were to take the opposite course and not meet one mischief by another. Would anyone think himself to be in his perfect mind if he were to return kicks to a mule or bites to a dog? "These creatures," you say, "know not that they are doing wrong." Then, in the first place, what an unjust judge you must be if a man has less chance of gaining your forgiveness than a beast! Secondly, if animals are protected from your anger by their want of reason, you ought to treat all foolish men in the like manner: for if a man has that mental darkness which excuses all the wrong-doings of dumb animals, what difference does it make if in other respects he be unlike a dumb animal? He has sinned. Well, is this the first time, or will this be the last time? Why, you should not believe him even if he said, "Never will I do so again." He will sin, and another will sin against him, and all his life he will wallow in wickedness. Savagery must be met by kindness: we ought to use, to a man in anger, the argument which is so effective with one in grief, that is, "Shall you leave off this at some time, or never? If you will do so at some time, how better is it that you should abandon anger than that anger should abandon you? Or, will this excitement never leave you? Do you see to what an unquiet life you condemn yourself? for what will be the life of one who is always swelling with rage?" Add to this, that after you have worked yourself up into a rage, and have from time to time renewed the cranes of your excitement, yet your anger will depart from you of its own accord, and time will sap its strength: how much better then is it that it should be overcome by you than by itself?

XXVIII.
If you are angry, you will quarrel first with this man, and then with that: first with slaves, then with f reedmen: first with parents, then with children: first with acquaintances, then with strangers: for there are grounds for anger in every case, unless your mind steps in and intercedes with you: your frenzy will drag you from one place to another, and from thence to elsewhere, your madness will constantly meet with newly-occurring irritants, and will never depart from you. Tell me, miserable man, what time you will have for loving? O, what good time you are wasting on an evil thing! How much better it would be to win friends, and disarm enemies: to serve the state, or to busy oneself with one's private affairs, rather than to cast about for what harm you can do to

somebody, what wound you can inflict either upon his social position, his fortune, or his person, although you cannot succeed in doing so without a struggle and risk to yourself, even if your antagonist be inferior to you. Even supposing that he were handed over to you in chains, and that you were at liberty to torture him as much as you please, yet even then excessive violence in striking a blow often causes us to dislocate a joint, or entangles a sinew in the teeth which it has broken. Anger makes many men cripples, or invalids, even when it meets with an unresisting victim: and besides this, no creature is so weak that it can be destroyed without any danger to its destroyer: sometimes grief, sometimes chance, puts the weakest on a level with the strongest. What shall we say of the fact that the greater part of the things which enrage us are insults, not injuries? It makes a great difference whether a man thwarts my wishes or merely fails to carry them out, whether he robs me or does not give me anything: yet we count it all the same whether a man takes anything from us or refuses to give anything to us, whether he extinguishes our hope or defers it, whether his object be to hinder us or to help himself, whether he acts out of love for someone or out of hatred for us. Some men are bound to oppose us not only on the ground of justice, but of honour: one is defending his father, another his brother, another his country, another his friend: yet we do not forgive men for doing what we should blame them for not doing; nay, though one can hardly believe it, we often think well of an act, and ill of the man who did it. But, by Hercules, a great and just man looks with respect at the bravest of his enemies, and the most obstinate defender of his freedom and his country, and wishes that he had such a man for his own countryman and soldier.

XXIX.
It is shameful to hate him whom you praise: but how much more shameful is it to hate a man for something for which he deserves to be pitied? If a prisoner of war, who has suddenly been reduced to the condition of a slave, still retains some remnants of liberty, and does not run nimbly to perform foul and toilsome tasks, if, having grown slothful by long rest, he cannot run fast enough to keep pace with his master's horse or carriage, if sleep overpowers him when weary with many days and nights of watching, if he refuses to undertake farm work, or does not do it heartily when brought away from the idleness of city service and put to hard labour, we ought to make a distinction between whether a man cannot or will not do it: we should pardon many slaves, if we began to judge them

before we began to be angry with them: as it is, however, we obey our first impulse, and then, although we may prove to have been excited about mere trifles, yet we continue to be angry, lest we should seem to have begun to be angry without cause; and, most unjust of all, the injustice of our anger makes us persist in it all the more; for we nurse it and inflame it, as though to be violently angry proved our anger to be just.

XXX.

How much better is it to observe how trifling, how inoffensive are the first beginnings of anger? You will see that men are subject to the same influences as dumb animals: we are put out by trumpery, futile matters. Bulls are excited by red colour, the asp raises its head at a shadow, bears or lions are irritated at the shaking of a rag, and all creatures who are naturally fierce and wild are alarmed at trifles. The same thing befalls men both of restless and of sluggish disposition; they are seized by suspicions, sometimes to such an extent that they call slight benefits injuries: and these form the most common and certainly the most bitter subject for anger: for we become angry with our dearest friends for having bestowed less upon us than we expected, and less than others have received from them: yet there is a remedy at hand for both these grievances. Has he favoured our rival more than ourselves? then let us enjoy what we have without making any comparisons. A man will never be well off to whom it is a torture to see any one better off than himself. Have I less than I hoped for? well, perhaps I hoped for more than I ought. This it is against which we ought to be especially on our guard: from hence arises the most destructive anger, sparing nothing, not even the holiest. The Emperor Julius was not stabbed by so many enemies as by friends whose insatiable hopes he had not satisfied. He was willing enough to do so, for no one ever made a more generous use of victory, of whose fruits he kept nothing for himself save the power of distributing them; but how could he glut such unconscionable appetites, when each man coveted as much as any one man could possess? This was why he saw his fellow-soldiers standing round his chair with drawn swords, Tillius Cimber, though he had a short time before been the keenest defender of his party, and others who only became Pompeians after Pompeius was dead. This it is which has turned the arms of kings against them, and made their trustiest followers meditate the death of him for whom and before whom they once would have been glad to die.

XXXI.
No man is satisfied with his own lot if he fixes his attention on that of another: and

this leads to our being angry even with the gods, because somebody precedes us, though we forget of how many we take precedence, and that when a man envies few people, he must be followed in the background by a huge crowd of people who envy him. Yet so churlish is human nature, that, however much men may have received, they think themselves wronged if they are able to receive still more. "He gave me the praetorship. Yes, but I had hoped for the consulship. He bestowed the twelve axes upon me: true, but he did not make me a regular consul. He allowed me to give my name to the year, but he did not help me to the priesthood. I have been elected a member of the college: but why only of one? He has bestowed upon me every honour that the state affords: yes, but he has added nothing to my private fortune. What he gave me he was obliged to give to somebody: he brought out nothing from his own pocket." Rather than speak thus, thank him for what you have received: wait for the rest, and be thankful that you are not yet too full to contain more: there is a pleasure in having something left to hope for. Are you preferred to everyone? then rejoice at holding the first place in the thoughts of your friend. Or are many others preferred before you? then think how many more are below you than there are above you. Do you ask, what is your greatest fault? It is, that you keep your accounts wrongly: you set a high value upon what you give, and a low one upon what you receive.

XXXII.
Let different qualities in different people keep us from quarrelling with them . let us fear to be angry with some, feel ashamed of being angry with others, and disdain to be angry with others. We do a fine thing, indeed, when we send a wretched slave to the workhouse! Why are we in such a hurry to flog him at once, to break his legs straightway? we shall not lose our boasted power if we defer its exercise. Let us wait for the time when we ourselves can give orders: at present we speak under constraint from anger. When it has passed away we shall see what amount of damage has been done; for this is what we are especially liable to make mistakes about: we use the sword, and capital punishment, and we appoint chains, imprisonment, and starvation to punish a crime which deserves only flogging with a light scourge. "In what way," say you, "do you bid us look at those things by which we think ourselves injured, that we may see how paltry, pitiful, and childish they are?" Of all things I would charge you to take to yourself a magnanimous spirit, and behold how low and sordid all these matters are about which we squabble and run to and fro till we

are out of breath; to anyone who entertains any lofty and magnificent ideas, they are not worthy of a thought.

XXXIII.
The greatest hullabaloo is about money: this it is which wearies out the law-courts, sows strife between father and son, concocts poisons, and gives swords to murderers just as to soldiers: it is stained with our blood: on account of it husbands and wives wrangle all night long, crowds press round the bench of magistrates, kings rage and plunder, and overthrow communities which it has taken the labour of centuries to build, that they may seek for gold and silver in the ashes of their cities. Do you like to look at your money-bags lying in the corner? it is for these that men shout till their eyes start from their heads, that the law-courts ring with the din of trials, and that jurymen brought from great distances sit to decide which man's covetousness is the more equitable. What shall we say if it be not even for a bag of money, but for a handful of coppers or a shilling scored up by a slave that some old man, soon to die without an heir, bursts with rage? what if it be an invalid money-lender whose feet are distorted by the gout, and who can no longer use his hands to count with, who calls for his interest of one thousandth a month, and by his sureties demands his pence even during

the paroxysms of his disease? If you were to bring to me all the money from all our mines, which we are at this moment sinking, if you were to bring to-night all that is concealed in hoards, where avarice returns money to the earth from whence it came, and pity that it ever was dug out—all that mass I should not think worthy to cause a wrinkle on the brow of a good man. What ridicule those things deserve which bring tears into our eyes!

XXXIV.

Come now, let us enumerate the other causes of anger: they are food, drink, and the showy apparatus connected with them, words, insults, disrespectful movements of the body, suspicions, obstinate cattle, lazy slaves, and spiteful construction put upon other men's words, so that even the gift of language to mankind becomes reckoned among the wrongs of nature. Believe me, the things which cause us such great heat are trifles, the sort of things that children fight and squabble over: there is nothing serious, nothing important in all that we do with such gloomy faces. It is, I repeat, the setting a great value on trifles that is the cause of your anger and madness. This man wanted to rob me of my inheritance, that one has brought a charge against me before persons whom I had long courted with great expectations, that one has coveted my mistress. A wish for the same things, which ought to have been a bond of friendship, becomes a source of quarrels and hatred. A narrow path causes quarrels among those who pass up and down it; a wide and broadly spread road may be used by whole tribes without jostling. Those objects of desire of yours cause strife and disputes among those who covet the same things, because they are petty, and cannot be given to one man without being taken away from another.

XXXV.
You are indignant at being answered back by your slave, your freedman, your wife, or your client: and then you complain of the state having lost the freedom which you have destroyed in your own house: then again if he is silent when you question him, you call it sullen obstinacy. Let him both speak and be silent, and laugh too. "In the presence of his master?" you ask. Nay, say rather "in the presence of the house-father." Why do you shout? why do you storm ? why do you in the middle of dinner call for a whip, because the slaves are talking, because a crowd as large as a public meeting is not as silent as the wilderness? You have ears, not merely that you may listen to musical sounds, softly and sweetly drawn out and harmonized: you ought to hear laughter and weeping, coaxing and

quarrelling, joy and sorrow, the human voice and the roaring and barking of animals. Miserable one! why do you shudder at the noise of a slave, at the rattling of brass or the banging of a door? you cannot help hearing the thunder, however refined you may be. You may apply these remarks about your ears with equal truth to your eyes, which are just as dainty, if they have been badly schooled: they are shocked at stains and dirt, at silver plate which is not sufficiently bright, or at a pool whose water is not clear down to the bottom. Those same eyes which can only endure to see the most variegated marble, and that which has just been scoured bright, which will look at no table whose wood is not marked with a network of veining, and which at home are loath to tread upon anything that is not more precious than gold, will, when out of doors, gaze most calmly upon rough and miry paths, will see unmoved that the greater number of persons that meet them are shabbily dressed, and that the walls of the houses are rotten, full of cracks, and uneven. What, then, can be the reason that they are not distressed out of doors by sights which would shock them in their own home, unless it be that their temper is placid and long-suffering in one case, sulky and fault-finding in the other?

XXXVI.

All our senses should be educated into strength: they are naturally able to endure much, provided that the spirit forbears to spoil them. The spirit ought to be brought up for examination daily. It was the custom of Sextius when the day was over, and he had betaken himself to rest, to inquire of his spirit: "What bad habit of yours have you cured to-day? what vice have you checked? in what respect are you better?" Anger will cease, and become more gentle, if it knows that every day it will have to appear before the judgment seat. What can be more admirable than this fashion of discussing the whole of the day's events? how sweet is the sleep which follows this self-examination? how calm, how sound, and careless is it when our spirit has either received praise or reprimand, and when our secret inquisitor and censor has made his report about our morals? I make use of this privilege, and daily plead my cause before myself: when the lamp is taken out of my sight, and my wife, who knows my habit, has ceased to talk, I pass the whole day in review before myself, and repeat all that I have said and done: I conceal nothing from myself, and omit nothing: for why should I be afraid of any of my shortcomings, when it is in my power to say, "I pardon you this time: see that you never do that anymore? In that dispute you spoke too contentiously: do not for the future argue with ignorant people: those who have never been taught are unwilling to learn. You reprimanded that man with more freedom than you ought, and consequently you have offended him instead of amending his ways: in dealing with other cases of the kind, you should look carefully, not only to the truth of what you say, but also whether the person to whom you speak can bear to be told the truth." A good man delights in receiving advice: all the worst men are the most impatient of guidance.

XXXVII.
At the dinner-table some jokes and sayings intended to give you pain have been directed against you: avoid feasting with low people. Those who are not modest even when sober become much more recklessly impudent after drinking. You have seen your friend in a rage with the porter of some lawyer or rich man, because he has sent him back when about to enter, and you yourself on behalf of your friend have been in a rage with the meanest of slaves. Would you then be angry with a chained house-dog? Why, even he, after a long bout of barking, becomes gentle if you offer him food. So draw back and smile; for the moment your porter fancies himself to be somebody, because he guards a door which is beset by a crowd of litigants; for the moment he who sits within is prosperous

and happy, and thinks that a street-door through which it is hard to gain entrance is the mark of a rich and powerful man; he knows not that the hardest door of all to open is that of the prison. Be prepared to submit to much. Is anyone surprised at being cold in winter? at being sick at sea? or at being jostled in the street? The mind is strong enough to bear those evils for which it is prepared. When you are not given a sufficiently distinguished place at table you have begun to be angry with your fellow-guests, with your host, and with him who is preferred above you. Idiot! What difference can it make what part of the couch you rest upon? Can a cushion give you honour or take it away? You have looked askance at somebody, because he has spoken slightingly of your talents; will you apply this rule to yourself? If so, Ennius, whose poetry you do not care for, would have hated you. Hortensius, if you had found fault with his speeches, would have quarreled with you, and Cicero, if you had laughed at his poetry, would have been your enemy. A candidate for office, will you resent men's votes?

XXXVIII.
Someone has offered you an insult? Not a greater one, probably, than was offered to the Stoic philosopher Diogenes, in whose face an insolent young man spat just when he was lecturing upon anger. He bore it

mildly and wisely. "I am not angry," said he, "but I am not sure that I ought not to be angry." Yet how much better did our Cato behave? When he was pleading, one Lentulus, whom our fathers remember as a demagogue and passionate man, spat all the phlegm he could muster upon his forehead. Cato wiped his face, and said, "Lentulus, I shall declare to all the world that men are mistaken when they say that you are wanting in cheek."

XXXIX.
We have now succeeded, my Novatus, in properly regulating our own minds: they either do not feel anger or are above it: let us next see how we may soothe the wrath of others, for we do not only wish to be whole, but to heal. You should not attempt to allay the first burst of anger by words: it is deaf and frantic: we must give it scope; our remedies will only be effective when it slackens. We do not meddle with men's eyes when they are swollen, because we should only irritate their hard stiffness by touching them, nor do we try to cure other diseases when at their height: the best treatment in the first stage of illness is rest. "Of how very little value," say you, "is your remedy, if it appeases anger which is subsiding of its own accord?" In the first place, I answer, it makes it end quicker: in the next, it prevents a relapse. It can render

harmless even the violent impulse which it dares not soothe: it will put out of the way all weapons which might be used for revenge: it will pretend to be angry, in order that its advice may have more weight as coming from an assistant and comrade in grief. It will invent delays, and postpone immediate punishment while a greater one is being sought for : it will use every artifice to give the man a respite from his frenzy. If his anger be unusually strong, it will inspire him with some irresistible feeling of shame or of fear: if weak, it will make use of conversation on amusing or novel subjects, and by playing upon his curiosity lead him to forget his passion. We are told that a physician, who was forced to cure the king's daughter, and could not without using the knife, conveyed a lancet to her swollen breast concealed under the sponge with which he was fomenting it. The same girl, who would have shrunk from the remedy if he had applied it openly, bore the pain because she did not expect it. ==Some diseases can only be cured by deceit==.

XL.
To one class of men you will say, "Beware, lest your anger give pleasure to your foes:" to the other, "==Beware lest your greatness of mind and the reputation it bears among most people for strength become impaired.== I myself, by Hercules, am scandalized at

your treatment and am grieved beyond measure, but we must wait for a proper opportunity. He shall pay for what he has done; be well assured of that: when you are able you shall return it to him with interest." To reprove a man when he is angry is to add to his anger by being angry oneself. You should approach him in different ways and in a compliant fashion, unless perchance you be so great a personage that you can quash his anger, as the Emperor Augustus did when he was dining with Vedius Pollio. One of the slaves had broken a crystal goblet of his: Vedius ordered him to be led away to die, and that too in no common fashion: he ordered him to be thrown to feed the muraenae, some of which fish, of great size, he kept in a tank. Who would not think that he did this out of luxury? but it was out of cruelty. The boy slipped through the hands of those who tried to seize him, and flung himself at Caesar's feet in order to beg for nothing more than that he might die in some different way, and not be eaten. Caesar was shocked at this novel form of cruelty, and ordered him to be let go, and, in his place, all the crystal ware which he saw before him to be broken, and the tank to be filled up. This was the proper way for Caesar to reprove his friend: he made a good use of his power. What are you, that when at dinner you order men to be put to death, and mangled by an unheard-of form of torture? Are a man's bowels to be torn asunder because your cup is broken? You must think a great deal of yourself, if even when the emperor is present you order men to be executed.

XLI.
If any one's power is so great that he can treat anger with the tone of a superior let him crush it out of existence, but only if it be of the kind of which I have just spoken, fierce, inhuman, bloodthirsty, and incurable save by fear of something more powerful than itself...let us give the mind that peace which is given by constant meditation upon wholesome maxims, by good actions, and by a mind directed to the pursuit of honour alone. Let us set our own conscience fully at rest, but make no efforts to gain credit for ourselves: so long as we deserve well, let us be satisfied, even if we should be ill spoken of. "But the common herd admires spirited actions, and bold men are held in honour, while quiet ones are thought to be indolent." True, at first sight they may appear to be so: but as soon as the even tenor of their life proves that this quietude arises not from dullness but from peace of mind, then that same populace respects and reverences them. There is, then, nothing useful in that hideous and destructive passion of anger, but on the contrary, every kind of evil, fire

and sword. Anger tramples self-restraint under-foot, steeps its hands in slaughter, scatters abroad the limbs of its children: it leaves no place unsoiled by crime, it has no thoughts of glory, no fears of disgrace, and when once anger has hardened into hatred, no amendment is possible.

XLII.
Let us be free from this evil, let us clear our minds of it, and extirpate root and branch a passion which grows again wherever the smallest particle of it finds a resting-place. Let us not moderate anger, but get rid of it altogether: what can moderation have to do with an evil habit? We shall succeed in doing this, if only we exert ourselves. Nothing will be of greater service than to bear in mind that we are mortal : let each man say to himself and to his neighbour, "Why should we, as though we were born to live forever, waste our tiny span of life in declaring anger against any one? why should days, which we might spend in honourable enjoyment, be misapplied in grieving and torturing others? Life is a matter which does not admit of waste, and we have no spare time to throw away. Why do we rush into the fray? why do we go out of our way to seek disputes? why do we, forgetful of the weakness of our nature, undertake mighty feuds, and, frail though we be, summon up all our strength to cut down other men? Ere

long, fever or some other bodily ailment will make us unable to carry on this warfare of hatred which we so implacably wage: death will soon part the most vigorous pair of combatants. Why do we make disturbances and spend our lives in rioting? fate hangs over our heads, scores up to our account the days as they pass, and is ever drawing nearer and nearer. The time which you have marked for the death of another perhaps includes your own."

XLIII.
Instead of acting thus, why do you not rather draw together what there is of your short life, and keep it peaceful for others and for yourself? ==why do you not rather make yourself beloved by everyone while you live, and regretted by everyone when you die?== Why do you wish to tame that man's pride, because he takes too lofty a tone with you? why do you try with all your might to crush that other who snaps and snarls at you, a low and contemptible wretch, but spiteful and offensive to his betters? Master, why are you angry with your slave? Slave, why are you angry with your master? Client, why are you angry with your patron? Patron, why are you angry with your client? Wait but a little while. See, here comes death, who will make you all equals. We often see at a morning performance in the arena a battle between

a bull and a bear, fastened together, in which the victor, after he has torn the other to pieces, is himself slain. We do just the same thing: we worry someone who is connected with us, although the end of both victor and vanquished is at hand, and that soon. Let us rather pass the little remnant of our lives in peace and quiet: may no one loathe us when we lie dead. A quarrel is often brought to an end by a cry of "Fire!" in the neighbourhood, and the appearance of a wild beast parts the highwayman from the traveller: men have no leisure to battle with minor evils when menaced by some overpowering terror. What have we to do with fighting and ambuscades? do you want anything more than death to befall him with whom you are angry? well, even though you sit quiet, he will be sure to die. You waste your pains: you want to do what is certain to be done. You say, "I do not wish necessarily to kill him, but to punish him by exile, or public disgrace, or loss of property." I can more easily pardon one who wishes to give his enemy a wound than one who wishes to give him a blister: for the latter is not only bad, but petty-minded. Whether you are thinking of extreme or slighter punishments, how very short is the time during which either your victim is tortured or you enjoy an evil pleasure in another's pain? This breath that we hold so dear will soon leave us: in the meantime, while we draw it, while we live among human beings, let us practise humanity: let us not be a terror or a danger to anyone. Let us keep our tempers in spite of losses, wrongs, abuse or sarcasm, and let us endure with magnanimity our shortlived troubles: while we are considering what is due to ourselves, as the saying is, and worrying ourselves, death will be upon us.

Footnotes

The hook alluded to was fastened to the neck of condemned criminals, and by it they were dragged to the Tiber. Also the bodies of dead gladiators were thus dragged out of the arena. The hook by which the dead bull is drawn away at a modern Spanish bull-fight is probably a survival of this custom.

Heroditus, iii, 34, 35

Seneca's own death, by opening his veins, gives a melancholy interest to this passage

Heroditus, iv, 84

Heroditus, vii, 38, 39

Plut. Dem. 27

Heroditus, iii, 17, sqq.

Heroditus, I, 189, 190

A mistake: Antigonus (Monophthalmus) was one of Alexander's generals

Acerbum = ἀώρου; the funeral of one who has been cut off in the flower of this youth

In point of time

Consul ordinarius, a regular consul, one who administered in office from the first of January, in opposition to consul suffectus, one chosen in the course of the year in the place of one who had died. The consul ordinarius gave his name to the year

It seems inconceivable that so small an interest, 1-1/5 per cent. per an., can be meant

Captatis, Madvig. Adv. II. 394

See "On Clemency," i. 18, 2

Manufactured by Amazon.ca
Bolton, ON